POLYAMORY
The New Love
Without Limits

SECRETS OF SUSTAINABLE
INTIMATE RELATIONSHIPS

Deborah M. Anapol, Ph.D.

IntiNet Resource Center
San Rafael, California

Published by
INTINET RESOURCE CENTER
POB 4322, SAN RAFAEL, CA 94913-4322
415/507-1739
Info@lovewithoutlimits.com
HTTP://WWW.LOVEWITHOUTLIMITS.COM

Printed in the United States of America. Printed on recycled paper.

POLYAMORY: THE NEW LOVE WITHOUT LIMITS reflects the personal
experience of the author. It is not intended to take the place of
professional help.

POLYAMORY: THE NEW LOVE WITHOUT LIMITS was previously
published in a different form in 1992 under the title LOVE WITHOUT
LIMITS.

*Publishers note: This book contains case histories derived from interviews
and research. The relevant facts have not been altered. However, names
and other identifying details have been changed to protect the privacy of the
individuals interviewed.*

Cover by Wolfgang Gersch, Meta Art Studios, San Anselmo, CA

Library of Congress Catalog Card Number: 91-77439

ISBN 1-880789-08-6

Revised Edition June, 1997. This is an original paperback.

10 9 8 7 6 5 4 3

CONTENTS

The facts. Definitions. Forms. What polyamory is *not*. How to share a lover.

Guidelines for responsible relationships. Is polyamory immoral?

Personality traits needed for polyamory. What about AIDS? New paradigm or old?

Know yourself. Heal yourself. Replace guilt and shame with self-acceptance and love. Master the art of communication. Open yourself to sexual energy. Let jealousy be your teacher. Choose a spiritual path. Look at the big picture.

CHAPTER 5: JEALOUSY AS GATEKEEPER   49

Nature versus nature. What is jealousy? Jealousy is not betrayal. Types of jealousy. What to do if you're feeling jealous What to do if your partner is feeling jealous Managing jealousy. Compersion.

CHAPTER 6: MAKING THE TRANSITION TO POLYAMOROUS RELATING   65

If you're single. If you've broken a monogamous commitment. If your partner has broken a monogamous commitment. How to ethically avoid monogamy without avoiding intimacy.

CHAPTER 7: COMING OUT POLY   79

Coming out as a process. Who is poly? The false dichotomy. Where have all the polys gone? The price we pay for staying in the closet. The rewards of coming out. Should I come out? How to come out. Coming out exercises. A coming out letter.

CHAPTER 8: FINDING YOUR TRIBE   95

A short history of the poly movement. Workshops and conferences. How to start a support group or salon. Finding others. Advertising. Meeting formats. Look Ma, No hands.

CHAPTER 9: BUILDING YOUR FAMILY   111

How to attract and select partners. Starting from square one. The birth of a group marriage. My own story. Common patterns. Enjoying the process.

ACKNOWLEDGMENTS

Although my name is listed as author of this book, it would be more accurate to say that I have been a vision-keeper and a synthesizer, gathering inspiration, knowledge and ideas from a wide variety of sources over the last decade.

I wish to thank the following people for their contributions to this work: Mary Beth Brangan, Al Crowell, Paul Glassco, James Heddle, John Holmdahl, Victor Gold, Nityama, Ryam Nearing and Brett Hill, Dr. James Prescott, and all those who commented on the previous edition for providing invaluable suggestions, criticism and encouragement.

Thanks also to the folks at the New Road Map Foundation, Loving More Magazine, my interviewees, clients, workshop participants and all domestic pioneers everywhere who are bravely exploring new relationship territory.

Thanks to my mother, Norma Anapol, for her continuing support, and to my daughter, Sonia Anapol, for tolerating years of fumbling as I began my quest for sustainable relationships.

Thanks to all those who generously gave permission to include their writing and their experiences, including those who preferred to remain anonymous.

Finally, my deepest gratitude to all of my lovers, past, present and future, who provided the inspiration for this book.

INTRODUCTION

*"In the early stages of a shift in patterns of morality,
people may feel unsettled, deviant, sinful, or out of
tempo with what they had formerly assumed to be true
and appropriate."*

June Singer, *The Energies of Love*

This book is addressed to the millions of men and women who are "failing" at traditional relationships and who feel guilty, isolated, and ashamed. It is addressed to the increasing numbers of single people who are sacrificing family for freedom. It is addressed to the thousands of intrepid souls who have matured beyond a blind acceptance of monogamy as the only legitimate form of sexualove and who are pioneering new relationship territory.

It is also addressed to the families, friends, and lovers of polyamorous people who may be puzzled, dismayed or even horrified by this poorly understood relationship orientation. Polyamory, like monogamy, can be expressed in both healthy and unhealthy ways. We hope that by describing what healthy polyamory looks like and feels like, we'll provide some criteria other than the number of partners for distinguishing between pathological and loving relationships.

Our culture desperately needs a new set of sexual ethics. We need a middle ground between the free love/do your own thing doctrine of the Sexual Revolution and outmoded lifelong monogamy. We need realistic guidelines that incorporate the highest wisdom from *all* of the diverse cultures which comprise today's global village.

The fact is that most of us *are* polyamorists at heart whether we are willing to admit it to ourselves or not. It is no accident that "serial monogamy," which is not really monogamy at all, is currently the most common relationship form in our culture. Serial monogamy can be viewed as being one step closer to who we really are. Unlike lifelong monogamy, it allows us to express our polyamorous nature while maintaining a monogamous fiction in which our multiple mates are separated by linear time. For some people this marriage-divorce-remarriage cycle remains the best solution.

But divorce increasingly appears to be more stressful and disruptive than first thought. The price that our children pay for our self-deception can be enormous. Although we all need the warmth and security of a nurturing family persisting over time, we must find ways to create sustainable intimate relationships which do not violate our intrinsic polyamorous nature. Where infidelity or the desire for broader sexual expression is the primary cause for the dissolution of a marriage, surely we can find more imaginative alternatives than divorce.

Our inherent capacity and desire for sexual intimacy with more than one partner is not the only reason why monogamous relationships fail. The reality is that many people are not sufficiently skilled at relating to one partner to be able to handle more than one. Some do choose polyamory to avoid facing fears or to escape intimacy. The point is that, ultimately, the clash between our non-monogamous nature and our monogamous tradition must begin to be seen as a legitimate reason to develop new forms of relationships.

There are many possible solutions to the current dilemma. This book explores only one option, which has been termed **polyamory** or **responsible nonmonogamy**. Not many years ago, few people had the necessary level of maturity to pursue this option. It was widely regarded as a utopian fantasy at best. But our society has rapidly grown beyond its adolescence, a response in part to the global crises which threaten the continuation of human life on this planet. *Polyamory, a viable alternative for those who wish to expand their social horizons to include multipartner relationships, is a concept whose time has come.*

Love is the most universal, the most tremendous
and the most mysterious of the cosmic forces.

PIERRE TEILHARD DE CHARDIN

Chapter 1

❧

WHAT *IS* POLYAMORY?

*"Most of you are jealous and possessive in your love. When
your love turns to possessiveness it makes demands. The
demands then alienate the loved one and you incorporate anger
and fear into the relationship. With these come bitterness and
aggression, and whether we speak of individual love
relationships or global interactions, what you call love, but is in
fact ownership and manipulation, takes over and the problems
then flow."*

Wayne Dyer, *Gifts from Eykis*

Our culture puts so much emphasis on monogamy that few
people realize they have a choice about how many
sexualoving partners they can have at one time. Even harder
to grasp is the idea that multi-partner relationships can be
stable, responsible, consensual, nurturing and long term.
Polyamory is not a synonym for promiscuity!

I myself didn't realize that polyamory was really a possibility
until I'd failed several times at the usual possessive and
dependent arrangement that commonly passes for love. As
time went on, I began to realize that, for me, monogamous
marriage was profoundly isolating and intolerably lonely,
partly because of the strict limits on whom I could love. My
husband at the time was only willing to love and accept me
if he could be sure that I loved and desired no one else.

In truth, however, I still cared deeply for all my past lovers
and sometimes encountered others to whom I felt strongly

attracted. Sure, I could suppress these feelings, but the bottom line was that in order to maintain my monogamous commitment I had to pretend to be someone other than who I really was. If I acknowledged being attracted to other men, my husband quickly let me know that I was out of line. Worse yet, as a trained observer of human behavior, he could easily detect any signs of attraction unless I was careful to cover them up. Our relationship didn't feel very intimate because it wasn't!

Another pattern I began to notice was that, after about four years of exclusive commitment to one partner, I would grow increasingly restless and dissatisfied. At first I thought the solution was to find a new and better partner. After several of these four year cycles, I realized I was just repeating the first stages of relationship over and over. Most of the long-term marriages I'd observed in my parents' generation seemed to go on automatic pilot after a few years, an alternative that didn't appeal at all. Nevertheless, I suspected that genuine intimacy could continue to unfold over many decades. In order to find out what was possible *later on* in a partnership, I realized I would have to find a way to *sustain* intimate relationships over time.

I knew that my real self wanted to give and receive unconditional love. I'd experienced this kind of total acceptance only outside the arena of marriage, in a few special friendships and in the contexts of psychotherapy and spiritual teaching. Next to this kind of genuine intimacy, most romantic liaisons seemed like protection rackets. I knew I was capable of loving more than one person at a time, so I assumed others must be, too. But strangely enough it never occurred to me that polyamory could coincide with marriage. So I decided that I was through with marriage and set off on a quest for sustainable intimacy.

It's been quite an amazing journey! It took me many years and one more marriage and divorce to realize that the secret to keeping any intimate connection alive is simply to be wholly authentic in every moment and to practice radical honesty. I've learned that relationships based on truth, self responsibility, and unconditional love can take many forms, but even small withholds will gradually erode any relationship. I've learned that it is indeed possible to love more than one person over many years. I call this lovestyle *responsible nonmonogamy* or *polyamory.*

THE FACTS

Most of us are not monogamous in the strict sense of the word. That is, we do not limit ourselves to one sexual partner for an entire lifetime. Census data reveal a global tendency for couples to divorce after four years of marriage.[1] And while many aspire to serial monogamy, or one partner at a time, national surveys repeatedly reveal that most Americans do not observe this rule very scrupulously, either. Statistics for married men and women reporting extramarital affairs, range from 37% to 70% for men and from 29% to 50% for women. And these proportions, particularly for women, increase as time goes on since more and more married women are working outside the home and consequently have more opportunities to encounter potential lovers. For single, unattached men and women the incidence of multiple, simultaneous relationships is undoubtedly even higher.

Unfortunately, the vast majority of multipartner relationships are neither ethical nor responsible! Lies, deceit, guilt, unilateral decisions and broken commitments are so commonplace in classic American-style nonmonogamy that responsible nonmonogamy may sound like an oxymoron.

When words like cheating, unfaithfulness, or adultery are used to represent a breakdown in sexual fidelity, divorce is likely to be the outcome.

Because so many of us have been raised to believe that it's simply not okay—with God, our parents or our partners—to be polyamorous, we fail to realize that we actually can include more than one sexualoving partner in our lives in an ethical and trustworthy fashion. We never realize the joy we can find in willingly sharing a lover. We never realize that we can design a lovestyle which is both nonmonogamous and responsible—one which can be positive for us, our loved ones, and the rest of the world—one which is also consistent with basic spiritual principles.

The bad news is that it won't necessarily be easy. But few people find monogamous relationships easy either. Still there is no denying that polyamory demands a good measure of maturity, self esteem, skill and commitment. If you're not willing to undertake the necessary preparation, polyamory is not for you. But if you value the depth, richness, excitement and evolutionary opportunities found here—enough to give it everything you've got—polyamory can be a very rewarding choice.

DEFINITIONS

So what is polyamory? The word *polyamory* comes from Greek and Latin roots meaning "many loves." I use it to describe the whole range of lovestyles which arise from an understanding that love can not be forced to flow, or not flow, in any particular direction. Love which is allowed to expand often grows to include a number of people. But to me, polyamory has more to do with an internal attitude of letting love evolve without expectations and demands than it does with the number of partners involved.

The term *polyamory* was first proposed by Church of All Worlds founders Oberon and Morning Glory Zell to replace the awkward expression *responsible nonmonogamy*. Cyberspace conversations via the Internet and the World Wide Web popularized its use all around the world over the last several years and helped bring it into general usage. However, we can better understand the meaning of polyamory by taking a look at the more descriptive words *responsible nonmonogamy*.

The *nonmonogamy* part of the equation, while difficult to say swiftly, is far easier to describe than the *responsible* part. Nonmonogamy used to mean having more than one spouse during your lifetime. Now it means having more than one sexual partner during the same time period. Whether the partners are married, legally or spiritually, and even how they interact sexually is not particularly relevant to our definition of nonmonogamy. We're simply speaking of all sexualoving relationships other than those limited to two people.

Singles who are dating more than one person are nonmonogamous, and couples who are sexual with others with or without the knowledge and consent of their primary partners are nonmonogamous. Three or more people who consider themselves to be married are nonmonogamous. Anyone with a circle of sexual friends is nonmonogamous. People who resume a sexual relationship with an ex-spouse or lover after finding a new partner are nonmonogamous. Even people who choose to have no sexualoving partners at all and remain celibate may be nonmonogamous.

Over the last several decades a number of words and phrases have been used to describe specific forms of responsibly nonmonogamous relationships. Some of these are polyfidelity, open marriage, open relationship, group marriage, multilateral marriage, intimate network, and triad. Other less specific terms include expanded family, nonexclusive relationship, intimate friendship and inclusive relationship.

Polyamory can include all of these, and it is not limited to any one of them. In fact, polyamory even includes couples who are currently monogamous, but who do not necessarily intend to remain exclusive forever. One thing all these types of relationships have in common is that they are *both* sexual *and* loving or *sexualoving* with *no separation between the sex and the love.* In other words, we're not talking about casual, indiscriminate sport sex.

Another thing that polyamorous relationships have in common is that they involve *consciously choosing* a particular lovestyle, rather than simply accepting the type of relationship which is most common in any given time and place. In polyamory you can design a relationship to fit your individual needs rather than automatically doing the same thing that everybody else does.

Polyamorous relationships may differ, however, in their basic intentions and approaches. Some polyamorous relationships resemble traditional monogamous marriage in their emphasis on creating an impermeable boundary around the group, operating according to a well defined set of rules (sometimes called a social contract), and expecting family members to replace individual desires with group agendas. I call this type of relationship *old paradigm* regardless of whether it is polyamorous or monogamous.

Other polyamorous relationships have a primary focus on using the relationship to further the psychological and spiritual development of the partners. These relationships tend to put more emphasis on responding authentically in the present moment, allowing for individual autonomy, and seeing loved ones as mirrors or reflections of oneself. These *new paradigm* relationships may also be either monogamous or polyamorous. Of course, many people these days are in transition and find themselves attempting to blend elements of old and new paradigms as well as monogamous and polyamorous lovestyles, but these distinctions are useful in clarifying the direction in which we wish to move.

Another dimension we must consider is the diversity of forms polyamory can take. In order to do this we need to have at our disposal language that enables us to communicate without resorting to conventional words that are judgmental, value-laden, or ambiguous. To that end, we propose the following terms.

Primary relationship. Lovers who are in a long-term, committed, marriage-type relationship are *primary partners.* Usually primary partners live together and share finances, parenting and decision making. Primary partners are not necessarily legally married, but they *are* bonded together as a family.

Secondary relationship. Secondary partners may also have a long-term, committed sexualoving relationship. But usually they live separately, have separate finances and see themselves as close friends rather than immediate family. Secondary partners may take on roles in each other's families similar to those of cousins, aunts and uncles in an extended family of blood relations.

Tertiary relationship. Lovers who spend time together only once in a while or for a brief time are *tertiary partners.* Their contact may be very intimate, but they are not an important part of each other's day to day life.

Polyamory can be practiced by any number of partners in any combination of primary, secondary, and tertiary relationships. While some polyamorous people object to the whole concept of hierarchies of commitment and rankings of love (as in the old Chinese practice of "number one wife"), varying levels of affinity can occur naturally. This diversity of form, along with the realization that identical forms may result from radically different dynamics, automatically creates a social environment different from our familiar homogeneous, avowedly monogamous culture. And this diversity challenges us to develop ethical guidelines which apply to the *quality* rather than the *form* of the relationship.

WHAT FORMS CAN POLYAMORY TAKE?

Open marriage or open relationship. These are both nonexclusive couple relationships, the main difference being whether the couple is married or not. In this scenario the partners have agreed that each can independently have outside sexualoving partners. A wide variety of ground rules and restrictions may apply.

Intimate network. This is a lovestyle in which several ongoing secondary relationships coexist. Sometimes all members of the group eventually become lovers. Sometimes individuals have only two or three partners within the group. The group can include singles only, couples only or a mixture of both. Another way to describe it would be as a circle of sexualoving friends.

Group marriage or multilateral marriage. These are both committed, long-term, primary relationships which include three or more adults in a marriage-like relationship. A group marriage can be open or closed to outside sexual partners.

Polyfidelity. A lovestyle in which three or more primary partners agree to be sexual only within their family. Additional partners can be added to the marriage with everyone's consent.

Triad. Three sexualoving partners who may all be secondary, all be primary, or two may be primary with a third secondary. It can be open or closed. A triad can be heterosexual or homosexual, but is often the choice of two same sex bisexuals and an opposite sex heterosexual.

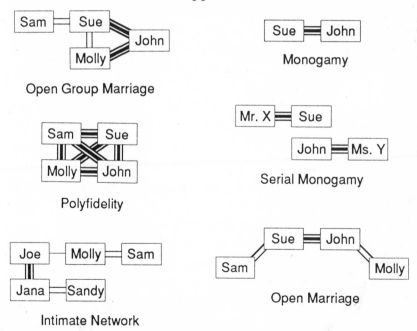

FORMS RESPONSIBLE NONMONOGAMY CAN TAKE.

Diagrams from the Polyfidelity Primer *by Ryam Nearing. Reprinted by permission from PEP, POB 4358, Boulder, CO 80306.*

WHAT POLYAMORY IS NOT

Perhaps you are wondering whether polyamory includes swinging? Superficially polyamory and swinging may appear to be the same. Admittedly there is some overlap. But while swinging is generally consensual and honest, the emphasis is usually on recreational sex rather than love and intimacy. My perception is that in swinging people tend to have sex first although they may become friends over time. In polyamory, people are more apt to become friends first although they may later get involved sexually. Swinging offers a maximum of sexual experience with a minimum of emotional involvement. In fact, many swinging couples make it a rule *not to fall in love* with their swinging partners. Consequently, I view swinging as a hybrid—monogamous on the love dimension while allowing specific nonmonogamous sexual experiences. However, some people start out experimenting with swinging but end up realizing they prefer polyamory -- and vice versa.

Swinging and polyamory also differ in that swinging has more of a commercial aspect. Large conventions, glossy magazines, tropical vacation tours, and a national network of swing clubs provide happy hunting grounds for those seeking sexual adventures. Polyamory is less a recreational activity than an alternative way of life which often encompasses economic, nutritional, and political alternatives. It is more likely than swinging to be inclusive of different sexual orientations. Grass roots polyamory support groups are more likely to focus on discussions and potluck dinners than sexy lingerie and the latest in dildos.

Polyamory is not philandering, and it is not a way to justify an uncontrollable urge to continually seek out new partners. Polyamory has nothing to do with proving that you're a real man or a real woman. It's not an excuse for having secret affairs or a means of establishing your independence. It is not simply sex for sex's sake, but an expression of your heart and soul.

How to Share a Lover

Sometimes it happens by design, sometimes it's unplanned. Sometimes, just maybe, it's one of those accidents of fate drawing us on into the unknown, on a journey into greater self-knowledge, greater integration and vastly expanded possibilities. Including more people will lead to an exponential increase in whatever is at the core of your attraction.

First, leave your preconceived expectations and judgments at the gate. That goes for excessive concern about what others will think, too. Learn to discriminate between form and substance. Happiness in a relationship comes from a shared experience of love, not from an external appearance or image of perfect couplehood. Ask yourself, how do I feel in this relationship? Trust your gut. If you have an inner certainty that you are engaged in a loving and joyous union, chances are your partners will agree with you. If you have doubts, check them out with an open-minded friend or unbiased therapist.

Second, do not tolerate deception, secrecy or lies. This doesn't mean you have to broadcast the most intimate details of your love to the world at large but cheating hurts everyone involved. Many people embark on multiple relationships without consulting their spouses or lovers because of their own guilt, jealousy or fear of rejection. In order to reap the benefits, it's essential that all parties have a clear and accurate understanding of what's going on. If you or your lovers won't risk telling the truth to all of your partners, do everybody a favor and stick to monogamy. It is best for your lovers to know and trust each other, that is, to have their own relationship, independent of you. It's also a good idea for all of you to spend some time together. If your lover refuses to participate in efforts at joint communication, try to identify the underlying obstacles. If there's no willingness to grow here, beware!

Third, clarify your own values and goals in life. Be consistent and communicate these to others. Don't mislead potential lovers by changing your intentions with your moods. If it's a priority for you to keep your life simple, predictable and uncomplicated, you probably won't be motivated to commit the necessary time and energy to maintaining inclusive relationships. More than one lover doesn't have to mean an endless marathon encounter, but it does require sensitivity, self-awareness, empathy and clear communication. If you don't already have these skills, you will have to develop them. Involvement in more than one intimate relationship tends to accelerate the process of personal growth and to intensify external activities. Seek out others who share your wants, needs and dreams. Don't try to force a round peg into a square hole. Make a list of the costs and benefits of your preferred relationship structure. Visualize it as you would like it to be. Ask yourself, how must I change in order for that to become a reality?

☙

Chapter 2

THE ETHICS OF POLYAMORY

"Secrecy is also withholding your true feelings from another person. If something someone said made you angry or if you see how a person can grow, and you don't want to tell either of them, that's secrecy . . . Anytime you withhold your natural self you help to construct a lie upon which the relationship is based. The relationship is then an illusion, because you never really know your true selves or each other."

Germane through Lyssa Royal

In many ways a responsible relationship is a responsible relationship, whether it is monogamous or not. But while you may be able to coast unconsciously with only one partner and avoid any major misunderstandings for a time, with polyamory it is absolutely crucial to consciously shape and refine your relationships. This is partly because polyamorous relationships are inherently more complex and partly because most of us lack experience and models for the application of familiar rules in this new context.

Polyamory by its very nature constitutes a challenge to our age-old conditioning and will undoubtedly stir up some discomfort. When these inevitable growing pains are intertwined with indignation arising from insensitive treatment by a thoughtless partner, it becomes much more difficult to trust the process and surrender to the valuable teachings polyamory can offer us. Undoubtedly, there will be times when it appears to you that your partner(s) are deliberately trying to hurt you. More than likely, they're just ignorant, as we all are when we venture into unfamiliar territory. Usually it's best to practice forgiveness, but don't combine that with forgetfulness. Instead, referring to the following guidelines may help you stay on track.

GUIDELINES FOR RESPONSIBLE RELATIONSHIPS

1. Consensus decision making

Perhaps the most basic requirement for an ethical and responsible relationship is that all partners freely agree to the terms and conditions governing the relationship. With monogamy it is relatively straightforward: both partners forsake all others. In polyamory, you have to decide when and how and to what extent multiple partners will be included. Likewise, in the old paradigm, it's simple. You make rules and you have penalties for breaking them. In the new paradigm it's even simpler, you allow whatever occurs to lead you to a greater understanding of yourself. But in between paradigms it's very complicated. We'll come back to this issue later on, but for now let's just say that most couples and other committed groupings find that *taking on new primary partners by consensus works best.*

Once you have ageed on some ground rules, you will need to negotiate any changes with all of your partners. For the polyamorous person, this means first of all being clear with yourself and your partners about what kinds of ground rules you want, preferably *before committing yourself to the relationship,* but better late than never. Don't make agreements you don't want to keep in order to preserve peace -- it's far better to let your conflicts surface now than to feel constrained and coerced later on. Be sure you inform yourself about the different options which are possible and learn to discern which may be appropriate for your situation.

You'll find polyamory is a lot like democracy—it works best with educated and involved citizens.

2. Honesty

Trustworthiness and dependability are two aspects of being responsible. It's hard to trust a person who lies, deceives or withholds information. Being scrupulously honest with yourself and your partners is especially important in polyamory because honest communication is the best way of handling the fears and jealousies which inevitably arise from time to time. Trust is based on the certain knowledge that your partners are giving you their unedited truth about their feelings and behavior. This gives your relationship the secure grounding it needs to remain comfortable when exploring polyamory. Hiding your polyamorous nature from prospective partners who may reject you out of hand may be tempting, but *it is not responsible.* In the long run it will backfire. Honesty includes being clear with your partners about your intentions and priorities. Of course, you must use good judgment about *when* to disclose something which may be difficult for your partners to hear, but never let your fear of hurting someone's feelings serve as an excuse for keeping secrets.

Withholding your true thoughts and feelings does just as much damage to you as to your partners by replacing intimacy with alienation and blocking the free flow of energy between you. Sooner or later you will find that the emotional withdrawal and resentment which invariably follow from not speaking your truth are deadening your love and your sexual response. Sustainable intimacy absolutely requires total honesty.

3. Mutual Caring

In polyamory, the well-being of all intimate friends must always be considered. Primary or marriage partners, secondary partners with whom you also have an ongoing sexualoving exchange and tertiary partners whom you may share with sexually only once or infrequently are all intimate friends who deserve your respect. For many of us, the question, "Does this relationship enhance and support everyone involved?" speaks to a necessary prerequisite that sincerely involves caring. At a bare minimum, a responsible relationship does no harm to any of the people involved. Consistent scapegoating, dumping of negative emotions and other abusive patterns have no place in a caring relationship. This doesn't mean that one may not be safely challenged, or asked to stretch or grow to accommodate the needs and desires of others. Nor does it mean pushing someone beyond their limits or convincing or coercing them to take unnecessary risks.

Caring also means conscientious attention to birth control and practices which minimize the spread of sexually transmitted diseases (STDs). While the risk of STDs is no greater in a closed multipartner relationship than in a monogamous one, it's obvious to everyone that, in an open relationship, one careless person can expose many others. And while an unplanned pregnancy can cause a crisis for a monogamous couple, it can easily destroy a polyamorous relationship by triggering primal jealousies at an inopportune time.

4. Commitment

The exact nature of your commitment to each other and to your relationships will depend on whether you have chosen primary, secondary, or tertiary relationships and whether you are working from an old paradigm or a new paradigm model. What everyone must realize is that meaningful sex creates a lifelong bond—lovers cannot be discarded like yesterday's garbage. If you are in an ongoing polyamorous relationship with one or more people, your partners need to know that you will not duck out of the relationship on a whim, or because you got scared, or because you've found someone else who wants you to be monogamous. Without a commitment to working to strengthen and enhance your existing relationships, adding new partners can only result in jealousy. Worse yet, without a commitment to something larger than yourselves, you may find it very difficult to function as a team.

Being committed to a relationship doesn't have to mean promising to stick around forever, no matter what. It does mean having a lifelong intention to support each other in whatever ways seem appropriate. So if you're just marking time until you find someone else you like better, you'll find it difficult to practice polyamory. The best way to avoid this dilemma is not to engage in marginal relationships. Should you find yourself sexually involved with someone who doesn't feel "right" to you, it's best to be honest with him or her about your lack of commitment. Give him or her the option to end the relationship if she or he is looking for something deeper. If you're in a primary relationship where any of your partners has veto power, your nonprimary partners need to know that you may discontinue the physical relationship without much warning, but you can still honor the bond between you.

Finally, if you are single and don't intend to have a primary relationship with anyone, you can still clarify the extent and limitations of the commitment you are willing to make to each of your partners. Be sure your partners know your commitment to remain single and polyamorous from the beginning and there will be less room for misunderstanding later on.

5. Integrity

Integrity means being able to keep commitments and is another aspect of being trustworthy. It requires *doing* whatever it is you *say* you are going to do, whether it's as mundane as washing the dishes or as central to the relationship as keeping an agreement to share your fears with your partner(s). It requires sufficient self-knowledge and self-acceptance to be aware of all the parts of yourself. Otherwise, one part of you is liable to make an agreement that some other part of you has no intention of keeping. This often happens to would-be monogamists. Once you've recognized and accepted your polyamorous self, and this part of you understands that you will honor it and protect its interests, your polyamorous self is usually more amenable to exercising some restraint and finding ways to express itself which will not harm others.

I learned the hard way that, in polyamory, integrity also means not making commitments to one partner that involve the cooperation of another partner without first getting agreement from everybody involved.

6. Respect For Each Individual's Boundaries

While it is important for primary partners to learn how to blend together as a single unit, it is also essential to honor each person's need to be an individual and to value the unique qualities and contributions each person brings to the relationship. While many people find it difficult to maintain their sense of self in a couple, losing one's self in a group can be an even scarier prospect.

A group which cannot allow for differences of opinion and cannot acknowledge each person's experience and intuition runs the risk of becoming a cult—or worse yet, an old-fashioned authoritarian family. Blurred boundaries lead to confusion, and confusion leads to discord and disease. A couple may be able to climb out of this morass, but three or more people had better avoid it from the beginning.

IS POLYAMORY IMMORAL?

Is *responsible nonmonogamy* a contradiction in terms? Is polyamory sinful by definition? Many people believe that the biblical injunction against adultery automatically makes polyamory morally unacceptable. But we must remember that many of the patriarchs were polygamists or had concubines. Father Abraham, warrior poet King David and wise King Solomon were all nonmonogamous. Were they committing adultery? Not at all. According to anthropologist Helen Fisher[1], author of *Anatomy of Love*, in Mosaic law only intercourse with a married woman was banned. The intention of the commandment against adultery was to protect the property rights of men to women, not to prohibit men from having multiple wives or lovers. Of course, things are different in our modern world, so let's explore the perspectives of some contemporary religious leaders and see what they have to say about ethical intimate relationships.

Episcopalian theologian Carter Heyward[2] emphasizes the importance of fidelity or faithfulness to our commitments, but says that faith involves "trusting that each of us is being honest with the other; that each knows and cares about the other on the basis of who [they] really are, rather than on the basis simply of who we might wish [them] to be; and that each desires the other's well-being."

Fidelity to our primary relational commitments does not require monogamy, asserts Dr. Heyward, but it does require that we be honest with each other and honor each other's feelings. Any sexual option, including monogamy, can be chosen in alienation as well as in fidelity.

Dr. Heyward points out that historically monogamy has benefited women and children by providing some economic security as it obligates men to provide for their families financially and has also served to protect women from men other than the husbands to whom they have belonged sexually.   Now that women in Western cultures have achieved some measure of equality, monogamy is no longer needed in the same way. Rather monogamy is fidelitous if it is chosen with the intention of building and sustaining trust in a relationship where extraordinary love and erotic power are present.

Heyward cautions that monogamy can shield spouses from their real feelings, fears, and yearnings and prevent growth in a relationship.   An "unexamined, static commitment to monogamy" can just as easily be used to destroy fidelity as to preserve it says Heyward. In other words, both polyamory and monogamy are morally neutral -- morality is a matter of how we conduct ourselves within our chosen lovestyle rather than adhering to any particular form.

Dr. Robert Francoeur, a married Catholic priest, proposes the concept of "flexible monogamy," in which sexual relationships with partners other than one's spouse are permitted within the context of a lifelong marriage.

Francoeur feels that flexible monogamy (or polyamory) is preferable to "serial polygamy," in which one has a series of short-lived monogamous marriages. Francoeur believes that flexible monogamy is more stable and better suited to the pressures of modern life.

Arthur Waskow, who teaches at the Reconstructionist Rabbinical College, points out that while the asserted norm for most Jews is sexual monogamy, the norm is often disobeyed in practice because it is untenable for many couples. He suggests that perhaps couples should make their own decisions about whether to be monogamous, and that sexual relations outside of marriage be considered adultery only if one of the partners betrays a *commitment* to monogamy.

He also points out that historically, in the Jewish tradition, it was legitimate for men to have more than one wife. But this practice was abandoned partly for the protection of women, and partly because of the contempt with which polygamy was viewed in the West. Perhaps there would be merit, he asserts, in ending the prohibition and allowing both men and women to take several mates. The question, he concludes, is one of whether *de facto* adultery is less dangerous than *de jure* polygamy.

Buddhist doctine or dharma focuses on the *effects* of our sexual acts, rather than the acts themselves, teaching that those acts which cause pain and harm to others or disturbance in ourselves should be avoided. According to the ancient Six Paramitas of the Bodhisattva, a moral person having sex with another must consider their own happiness, that of their companion and of the third person who will be most affected by the situation. If these three people can be satisfied, then polyamory is not adultery and is completely acceptable.[3]

The 19th century mystic Baha'u'llah, founder of the Baha'i faith, was a product of the Moslem culture in which men only are permitted more than one wife and where the status of woman was—and is—abysmally low. He had other concerns about multiple marriages as a staunch advocate of the rights of women and the importance of the family. He believed, as the *Koran* teaches, that in an ethical and moral marriage each spouse must be treated exactly equally. He condemned polygamous marriage on the grounds that this condition was rarely met. In so doing, he became perhaps the first spokesperson for modern polyamory.

The guidelines for polyamory and the contemporary religious perspectives summarized above both suggest that in evaluating the morality of any lovestyle it is less important to blindly follow a particular rule or custom than it is to ask:

> *Does this relationship have a positive effect on those who are in it, on any children produced by it, and on the rest of the world?*

> *Does this relationship effectively serve the basic functions of family life?*

> *Is this relationship consistent with my deepest values?*

Those of us choosing polyamory can answer these questions with a resounding *YES!* as we shall see in the next chapters.

Chapter 3

ᘓ

IS POLYAMORY RIGHT FOR ME?

*"Sex is a sacrament, not a prison. While monogamy can be a
beautiful, even sacred bond, it might not be the agreement that
best suits everyone. Our thinking that monogamy is inherently
a nobler arrangement than any other has created a nation of
hypocrites -- which is what we've become."*
Marianne Williamson, A Woman's Worth

If you are like most people in our culture, you grew up
assuming that you would eventually enter a heterosexual,
monogamous marriage. You probably never thought about
whether you wanted a lifestyle which included multiple
sexual partners. If your family life was very unhappy, you
may have decided not to get married at all. If your mother
or father had love affairs which damaged or even destroyed
their marriage, you may have vowed never to do this
yourself. Or you may have unconsciously decided to model
yourself after them.

Perhaps you found yourself reluctant to "finally decide to
pick up on one and let the other one ride," as the Loving
Spoonful sang in a hit song from the sixties. Perhaps you
read books like Robert Heinlein's *Stranger in a Strange Land* or
Robert Rimmer's *Harrad Experiment* which described fantasy
worlds where loving more than one person was possible,
and you found the idea attractive. But chances are you had
no awareness of choosing from the whole range of lovestyle
designs because you knew of only one legitimate one–

monogamous marriage. Take it or leave it was the name of the game for you.

Most human beings are not naturally monogamous for life. Statistically speaking, chances are that you're not either. But this doesn't necessarily mean that polyamory is the right choice for you. Making this decision involves examining a complex set of interacting factors and in the end, you are likely to find that there are so many unknowns, you simply have to "follow your bliss." Nevertheless, you can begin to get a handle on whether polyamory is right for you by considering the personal characteristics which seem best suited for this lovestyle and then asking yourself if these are traits which you possess—or want to acquire. Let's survey some of them.

A talent for intimate relationships. Some people have a gift for music, others are natural athletes. If you have a gift for getting close to people, for giving and receiving affection, if you're empathic and compassionate and enjoy sharing life's pleasures and sorrows with a group of people, then you have a *talent for relating intimately.* Without this talent, it can be a struggle to handle even one meaningful relationship. But people who are gifted in this way find they have the capacity for opening their heart to many with no ill effects. This talent sometimes leads people into one of the "helping professions"—nursing, psychotherapy, teaching, or social work. Such people also make good managers—and good parents.

High self esteem. It takes plenty of self-confidence to be willing to share your lovers with others, secure in the knowledge that you will not measure up short in comparison. Even more basic is a sense of your own worth which doesn't depend on anyone else's acceptance. This quality makes it possible to face the unknown territory of multiple relationships without excessive fears. It transforms problems into challenges. It equips you to validate yourself for choosing a lovestyle that others may not understand.

A good juggler. Some people function best doing one thing at a time with no distractions. Others find it easy to track several different processes at once by shifting back and forth as needed. Such people often *prefer* the variety and stimulation of having a broader focus. If you can juggle tasks, projects and changing demands, you probably also have the ability to juggle people–without dropping the ball.

A love of intensity. Multiple partners means more activity, more interaction, more energy, more interests, more change, more obligations, more coordination, more everything! Monogamous couples may find that, in between developmental crises and periods of rapid growth, there are long uneventful stretches, but with more people involved *something* is always happening with *someone.* Fortunately, more partners also means that you're able to spend time alone while your partners are together. But if you're all spending some time together, you'll find that just the combined presence of an intimate, no barriers group of people creates a definite intensity of its own. If you like intensity, it's heaven. If you don't, you'll wish you had stayed with monogamy.

Appreciation for diversity. Every group or family needs to come to terms with differences among its members. If you want everyone in your intimate circle to be exactly like you in order to feel comfortable, you'll be increasing your frustration by expanding that circle to include more people. It's important to choose partners who share basic values, but part of the joy of polyamory is recognizing and honoring each person's uniqueness.

Interpersonal skills. Multipartner relationships can be emotionally complex. You don't have to be perfect, but you can get very confused very fast without a good grasp of your own personal dynamics and some awareness of how groups function. The better your skills at communicating, negotiating, nurturing, asserting yourself, piercing your own—and others—defenses, the less trouble you'll have.

Ability to be flexible, creative and spontaneous. With a couple, it's possible to maintain at least an illusion of control and predictability. As anyone who has children knows, chaos better describes the complexities of multiple, interacting individuals. Mature adults can hopefully regulate themselves better than children, but polyamory will probably present a threat to those who feel a strong need for control. Furthermore, flexibility makes it possible for a group of adults to share power through situational leadership. That is, Jane can handle financial matters while Harry rules the kitchen and Pat takes care of the cars.

A sex positive attitude. You may be attracted to the idea of multiple partners because you have a high sex drive, or because you're bisexual, or because you are looking for a solution to a mismatch in the level of sexual desire between you and your partner. Whatever your particular situation, it's likely that sexual considerations are involved. And whatever your particular situation, it's unlikely that you'll be comfortable with an expanded sexual environment unless you're generally comfortable with and able to accept your own and other people's sexuality.

An independent streak. If it's important to you to maintain a sense of yourself as an individual in addition to any group or couple identity you might adopt, then you may feel more comfortable with a relationship contract which acknowledges the possibility that you can become intimate with someone in addition to your existing partners. How these attractions are dealt with is another matter, but the bottom line is that you don't have to pretend that certain desires don't exist.

A team spirit. Independence alone makes it difficult to cooperate with others over time. But combined with a team spirit, it sets the stage for a "win-win" style which can create a powerful synergy. If you are willing to work for the good of the whole group, and if you recognize that this will benefit you more in the long run than an exclusive focus on your own private agenda, then you're a good candidate for polyamory.

A commitment to personal and spiritual growth. Polyamory, especially in the early stages, is a demanding lovestyle. The challenges of relating intimately to more than one partner at a time will certainly accelerate your own development. This can be an asset or a liability, depending upon your motivations. If you wish to use your relationships in order to become more conscious of your own dysfunctional patterns and buried feelings so that you can release them and increase your capacity for intimacy, polyamory offers you an unparalleled opportunity to do so. Nothing will bring your "stuff" to the surface more quickly than involvement with several intimate partners at once. Nothing will open your heart and activate your fears more intensely. If you welcome the chance to work on yourself in this way, then polyamory may be for you.

WHAT ABOUT AIDS?

Many people these days are fearful of choosing a polyamorous lovestyle because of concerns about exposing themselves to AIDS or to sexually transmitted diseases such as herpes which can be unpleasantly chronic if not life-threatening. In recent years government agencies and the media have tended to overemphasize the threat of disease for the average citizen to the point where you may unconsciously equate sex with death. This fear process probably poses a much greater threat to your health than responsible nonmonogamy.

If fear of disease is the only factor motivating your choice of lovestyle, consider this. A closed circle, whether of two or six or twenty, healthy, trusted partners can make polyamory just as "safe" as monogamy, perhaps more so since the couple who have sworn to be monogamous may be more likely to lie about outside affairs and less likely to frankly discuss their sexual histories with prospective lovers than those who are openly polyamorous.

A safe sex circle or condom commitment can be entered into by any number of partners who first take appropriate steps to see that they are free of communicable diseases and then agree not to have "unprotected sex" outside the group and not to engage in other high risk behaviors such as intravenous drug use. Each group will have to define what specific behaviors fall into the category of unprotected sex. If anyone slips up they report this to the group and are then quarantined until they can renew their clean bill of health.

Of course, it's also possible to share sexual energy without penetration or exchanging bodily fluids, and this is also a good alternative to fear-based monogamy.

The bottom line is that creating a healthy body, mind, and spirit will offer you more real protection than relying on one or more partners who may make promises they fail to keep. A highly functional immune system, a sex positive attitude, and your own ability to discern when and with whom it's appropriate to engage with sexually offer you the security you need to love freely in our modern world. Exercise good judgement, but don't let exaggerated fears keep you from listening to your heart.

NEW PARADIGM OR OLD?

As we discussed in Chapter One, you may also want to think about whether you want a new paradigm or an old paradigm style of relating. In general, old paradigm relationships are intended to maximize security, stability, predictability, and control. These qualities can be difficult to attain even in monogamous relationships, so be prepared for some additional challenges if you're choosing old paradigm polyamory.

Old paradigm relationships usually work best when one person takes a strong leadership role and when everyone involved enjoys operating according to specific rules. With old paradigm relationships total honesty is considered less important than protecting one another from unpleasant truths and continued love and acceptance is usually conditional on meeting your partner's needs. Old paradigm lovestyles may be a good choice for people who like a lot of structure and who want to stick with familiar forms. For example, couples who are cautiously exploring new alternatives but are anxious to protect their primary bond often feel more comfortable with the old paradigm.

New paradigm relationships appeal more to people who are willing to take a leap into the unknown and whose desire to transcend ego exceeds their desire to play it safe. In the new paradigm, unconditional love and mutual empowerment are ideals toward which partners aspire. Choosing the new paradigm means giving up attachment to having your relationship adhere to a particular picture you may have of "how it's supposed to be." You must be prepared to let the right form emerge from the truth of your beingness.

Unfortunately, these two belief systems for relationship are not compatible with each other, so while many people are attracted to elements of both paradigms, this is one situation in which you're probably going to find it's a package deal. Most people find that attempts to blend paradigms result in abundant blame, anger, and confusion instead of abundant love.

My own bias is that polyamory works much more smoothly when it grows out of new paradigm principles. In fact, many of the failures which have discouraged polyamorous explorers in the past can be traced to attempts to enforce old paradigm rules while expecting new paradigm results or to add more partners while maintaining old paradigm beliefs. But don't take my word for it. Look within and see which paradigm feels right for you.

Chapter 4

ᎧᏃ

EIGHT STEPS TO
SUCCESSFUL POLYAMORY

*"If a new world view is in the making, as I believe it is,
sexuality has not yet been incorporated into that vision.
Current sexual practice can no longer be explained by the old
theories and we do not yet understand it in the light of the new
ones. Racing ahead of history, we now find ourselves in a new
territory."*

June Singer, *The Energies of Love*

Multipartner relationships are inherently more complex and
demanding than monogamous ones. The difficulties are
compounded by the fact that those interested in polyamory
are operating outside the norms of our culture and venturing
into unfamiliar territory—without a road map!
Consequently, strength derives from overcoming the kinds
of obstacles and hardships pioneers have always faced. In
our age there are few geographic frontiers left, but the
challenges of exploring new ways of relating intimately are
no less demanding than those faced by the intrepid explorers
who risked sailing over the edge of a supposedly flat world.

Fortunately, we have at our disposal many useful tools for
personal and spiritual growth and for communing with each
other, which are easily adapted to our purposes. Select the
ones which appeal to you, and practice them until they're
second nature. Be sure that the path you select addresses
the seven basic issues outlined below.

STEP 1: KNOW YOURSELF

Before you can select partners and lovestyles which will be compatible with your unique constellation of needs, desires, traits, and personal history, you will need a good idea of who you are and what you want. This may seem obvious, but a surprising number of people leap into unexamined relationships on the basis of sexual attraction or childhood conditioning. They don't realize they can *design a lovestyle* from a whole menu of relationship options. Not surprisingly, many of these off-the-rack relationships turn out to be disappointing.

First ask yourself, what would my ideal relationship be like? Some people respond to this question by listing physical characteristics which they find sexually exciting. If you can't get beyond this level, perhaps swinging would be of more interest to you than polyamory. In a sustainable relationship, the partners need to share a vision of how they will interact, and they need to agree on basic values and life goals. This needn't go so far as to specify how many men and how many women should live in what kind of house. However, you should consider whether you are open to having one or more *primary* partners and whether you want *open* or *closed* relationships. Your design will certainly change over time. If you and your partners have made choices based on shared values and goals, you will find it easier to modify the form later on.

What are your primary motivations for being in a relationship? Nearly everyone hopes to find companionship and sexual intimacy. But is personal or spiritual growth a priority? Do you want partners who share your level of maturity or are you willing to have a teacher/student dynamic? Do you want to raise children? Do you want someone to share a special interest, business or avocation? Multipartner relationships in which everyone has a common mission have the most potential for synergy. And this requires knowing what your life purpose *is*.

What other requirements do you have? What kind of financial arrangements do you want? What kinds of health and nutritional issues are important to you? Are you a homebody or do you like to be on the go constantly? Do you want to live in the city, the country or somewhere in between? Do you want your partners to share your spiritual or religious preference? Is cultural, ethnic, or racial background a consideration?

Some people are drawn to polyamory because of the possibilities of combining some of these seemingly opposite choices. For example, an expanded family could support *both* city *and* country residences. But if you have strong preferences on any of these basic parameters, you can avoid a lot of conflict by choosing partners who share your tastes.

Choosing partners with complementary personality traits also makes for a more stable relationship. For some dimensions, a person with similar traits will be compatible. For other dimensions, opposite traits will work better. In most cases, the flexibility to shift from one pole to the other is extremely helpful. For example, first-born or only children usually are inclined to take a dominant position with others. Three first-borns who stubbornly insist on calling the shots will find themselves in a constant power struggle. Conversely, three submissive second-borns may suffer from chronic indecisiveness. On this dimension, opposites combine well. And a mix of dominant and submissive types can give everyone the opportunity to learn from each other and experiment with both styles.

On the other hand, introverts will find it easy to relate to other introverts, while extroverts may seem like creatures from another planet. There may be a polar attraction, but on this dimension opposites *do not* combine well. However, in a multipartner relationship a person who has some introverted and some extroverted qualities may be able to serve as a bridge between those who are less evenly balanced.

You can discover these principles by trial and error, but it's a lot faster and less painful to take advantage of existing psychological knowledge. If you don't take the trouble to learn about your own personality and any dysfunctional ways of coping that you might have picked up, you'll find it hard to maintain a relationship with even one person. When multiple partners are involved, a negative spiral can quickly blow the relationship apart.

STEP 2: HEAL YOURSELF

Multipartner relating is demanding enough without adding disruptive chronic problems. Addictions, ill health and immaturity all burden a relationship, sometimes fatally.

If you are abusing drugs or alcohol, you'll need to do something about your addiction before you'll be fully available to one partner, let alone to more. Addictions to work, melodrama, food, sex, conflict or just being in control also interfere with your capacity for relationships. Be honest with yourself. You may be able to hide out in a "co-dependent" relationship with one partner, but the odds are against it here. Take care of your addictions *before* taking on polyamory.

If your health is unstable in any way, take the time to understand why and learn what you can do to improve it. You'll need all the energy and stamina you can muster to fully enjoy a polyamorous lovestyle. Some people are attracted to polyamory as a way of coping with a physical disability. Supportive partners *can be* an invaluable resource, but you must first make the effort to function at your highest level of health.

Illness and addictions are two major barriers to intimacy. The third is harder to pinpoint, but is sometimes referred to as *immaturity*. A monogamous couple may find it difficult, but still possible, to maintain a relationship in which they simply deny aspects of themselves or each other. An unspoken contract based on dependency and control often protects the immature partners from having to grow—and from healing childhood traumas which have impeded their growth. Adding more partners can upset the fragile balance of such a relationship.

This is especially true when either partner is sexually wounded. If your sex life is less than optimal because of childhood abuse or other past negative experiences, inexperience or lack of information, physical difficulties, or simple inhibition you will naturally be threatened by the prospect of including a more sexually adequate partner. Undertaking your own sexual healing will allow you to feel less competitive because you will be more secure internally.

Multiple partner relationships work best in an atmosphere of unconditional love. And that requires a sense of wholeness and maturity. If you are preoccupied with having your partners fill your needs, you'll find it hard to love without a lot of strings attached. If you are depending on your partners to make you happy, chances are you'll find yourself feeling possessive. Unconditional love can certainly be present in a dyad, but as a sexualove relationship grows *beyond* two partners, it becomes essential to successful relationships.

Develop your own capacity for tolerating uncertainty, managing your moods and your sexual energy, nurturing yourself, staying in touch with your feelings without being overwhelmed by them, thinking clearly and understanding yourself. If you can do these things, you will naturally experience an inner completeness which flows easily into deep intimacy and a readiness to merge with others.

STEP 3: REPLACE GUILT AND SHAME WITH SELF-ACCEPTANCE AND LOVE

One of the most formidable obstacles you will encounter is your own guilt and shame. Because most of us are taught from infancy that it's wrong to have more than one lover at a time—or even more than one best friend—we usually try to deny or avoid admitting that *we want to have multiple partners.* You will have overcome visions of yourself as a sinner, hedonist, or overgrown teenager before you're prepared to exercise your right to choose polyamory.

Even if you don't believe that polyamory is sinful, you may be concerned about the disapproval of others. Depending upon where you live, the type of work that you do, and the kind of family you were raised in, this may or may not be a *realistic* fear. It takes high self esteem to permit yourself to make an unpopular choice.

The natural tendency of guilt-ridden people is to behave secretively and surreptitiously. This makes it difficult to be open and honest with prospective partners. If you don't feel good about being polyamorous, you can't expect others to go along with you, let alone enthusiastically support you. In fact, if you're not comfortable with yourself, you're more than likely to provoke abundant confirmation that you are indeed an evil, selfish creature who wants to "have your cake and eat it too."

This is one reason why it's important to be a *responsible* non-monogamist. If you've lied, cheated or deceived your partners in the past, forgive yourself, turn over a new leaf, and don't ever again give yourself grounds for feeling guilty about the way you're treating your partners. Healthy guilt is a message to yourself that you're doing something harmful or *not* doing something helpful. If you correct the problem, the guilty feeling goes away. Neurotic guilt is an ever-present monkey on your back that frequently results from simply asserting your right to be who you are. If you are careful to behave ethically and to learn to pay attention to the results of your actions, you won't fall into the trap of confusing polyamory with irresponsibility. Everyone involved should benefit from polyamory.

Learn to forgive yourself, accept yourself, love yourself. Then you'll be able to give these gifts to your partners, too. For many people this will involve *reparenting* yourself or *working with your inner child.* You may also find there is a spiritual dimension to this process. Many excellent books, tapes and seminars are available to assist you in learning to love yourself.

STEP 4: MASTER THE ART OF COMMUNICATING

There is an old children's game in which one person whispers a secret to the person on their right who in turn whispers it to their neighbor, and so on around the circle.

Typically, the message is completely garbled by the time it gets around the circle. This game is not very amusing, however, when it becomes a metaphor for communication in your most intimate relationships.

Co-ordinating practical details like schedules and logistics can be challenging when more than two people are involved. If the message is not clearly given to begin with, it's bound to get distorted. The more people it must reach, the greater the possibilities for confusion. Emotionally laden communication about sexual issues, hurt feelings and anger, or even praise, admiration and other favorable feedback has even more potential for miscommunication.

To create positive rather than negative synergy, you need to ensure that all the communication channels are open and that clear messages are being transmitted. Clear communication starts with being clear and unambiguous about what you want to say. Take responsibility for saying what you want and, if you have any doubt about whether you've been heard correctly, ask your partners to repeat it back to you. If it's not quite right, try again, and don't stop until you're satisfied that you are being understood.

This technique is especially useful when you're exploring new and unfamiliar feelings or if you're making an unusual request. If you feel caught in the middle between two partners, talk to both of them together. Insist that all parties involved talk directly to each other rather than relying on intermediaries. When there *are* problems in your relationship, they can be dealt with much better once they're out in the open.

Communicating also involves *responding* or giving feedback to your partners. For instance, don't assume that your partners *know* that you feel left out or pressured. Two people may become so sensitive to each other's emotional states that they're tempted to rely on "mind reading" instead of telling each other when they need something. This is a dangerous practice for couples, but it can be disastrous when more people are involved. Don't risk it!

Clear transmission is only half of the art of communicating. *Listening* is equally critical. You can improve the quality of listening by creating an optimal listening environment. This means eliminating distractions, setting aside sufficient time, and generally focusing attention on each other before you launch into some important revelation. Try to put aside your own agenda or your need to "fix it." Concentrate on hearing *and feeling* your partner's message. Often it is the *feeling tone*, rather than the words, which most needs to be heard. Again, if you're not sure you understand, repeat what you heard and ask for verification.

If this is a three-or-more-way conversation, you may find that one person will be able to "translate" for another, but make *sure* the translator does not distort the original message. Also, be especially careful to stay with the primary issue; it's easy to go off on tangents in a stimulating group conversation. Many people find that having one designated speaker at a time works best, with listeners interjecting only to ask for clarification until the speaker is done or the topic is complete. If you sense an unspoken request, ask the speaker to make it explicit before moving on to the next person or subject.

STEP 5: OPEN YOURSELF TO SEXUAL ENERGY

A polyamorous lifestyle involves much more than sexuality, but the sexual aspects are powerful because of the cumulative effect of having multiple partners. This is true even if most of the sexual activity is limited to two people at one time, but powerful sexual dynamics are especially apparent in group sexual experiences.

Many people are unprepared for higher intensity sex and consequently find the idea of more than one lover frightening, threatening or intimidating as well as stimulating and exciting. In fact, the same state of physical arousal might be interpreted as either pleasurable, overwhelming or anxiety-producing, depending upon your mind set. The greater the flow of sexual energy, the more likely you are to feel that you are losing control of the situation.

In addition, if you've been strongly conditioned to allow sexual intimacy with only one partner with whom you are exclusively "mated," the idea of multiple partners may seem alien or even repulsive. Some people have internalized our culture's overall sex negative attitude and find it hard to overcome a distaste for sex even with one legitimate partner. For others, the difficulty can be traced to a tendency to become emotionally dependent upon or possessive about a sexual partner. Some people attempt to overcome their dependency or possessiveness by always having several partners and keeping them all at arms length. This strategy may work for awhile, but it is at the expense of developing deep, bonded, intimate relationships and tends to give polyamorous people a reputation for preferring to stay superficial. Fortunately, there are other ways to comfortably keep your balance with one or more partners.

Any tool for increasing your flow of life force—variously called *chi, prana,* or *kundalini*—and opening your energy centers or *chakras* will help prepare you for multipartner sex. General practices such as yoga, meditation, certain kinds of dance, centering and grounding exercises or relaxation training can be very effective. Internal martial arts training such as T'ai Chi Ch'uan, Ch'i Kung or Aikido have the additional benefit of heightening your sensitivity to a partner. All of these kinds of energy work will improve your overall health and sense of well-being, so you can only gain by finding one you like and making it part of your daily routine.

Tantric, Taoist, alchemical, and native American traditions all offer teachings about how to access heightened energy states and expanded consciousness through specific sexual practices. For convenience, we'll refer to them all as *tantra* in the discussion below. This knowledge has been carefully guarded through centuries of direct transmission from teacher to student (or *tantrika*) and by sketchy, heavily coded writings. In recent years the teachings have become much more accessible to the general public. A variety of books, tapes, and seminars on tantric practices are now available. For more information on my own tantra workshops, write to me at the address in the back of this book.

Tantric practice provides an important groundwork for polyamory. Since it can be learned alone or by either a heterosexual or homosexual couple, it is available to anyone who desires a heightened sexual experience regardless of sexual or relationship orientation. In fact, tantra became increasingly popular in the '80s as monogamous couples desperately sought ways to keep their sex lives fulfilling. The tantric concept of sex as a sacred act creates a much more accepting attitude toward sexuality for everyone, but tantric training offers special advantages to the polyamorous.

One contribution is the tantric focus on *making love to the god or goddess within your partners.* This focus lifts us out of our usual over-identification with the ego or personal self, and makes it easier to see ourselves and our partners as different manifestations of a single universal male or female. In tantra, each partner experiences union with the cosmos and consequently with each other. This shift in perspective both adds depth to your connection and lessens jealousy, dependency, and possessiveness. In tantric culture there are many gods and many goddesses, and all are valued for their unique qualities. There is no need to eliminate one to worship another since all is One anyhow.

Tantric practice also puts a lot of emphasis on reconnecting the sexual and the heart centers. Many men benefit by learning to channel their sexual energy to open a well-defended heart, and many women benefit by learning to channel their love energy to awaken their frozen genitals. Both sexes can learn to stay out of pure lustful or pure asexual states which can be easily triggered by group encounters—and which can discourage potential partners.

Tantra can provide effective techniques for the man who wants to satisfy more than one woman. By learning to *separate orgasm from ejaculation*, any man is able to match women's innate capacity for multiple and continuous orgasm. Tantra also teaches a style of lovemaking that most women find much more enjoyable than that usually practiced in our culture. Both genders may find that once they are fully awakened sexually, they will have a greater sexual desire than they experienced previously.

Finally, tantra provides important training in learning to direct the flow of sexual energy and in keeping your mind from interfering with your sexual exchange. These are useful skills for solo and coupled sex, but they are critical for an optimal group sexual experience. If you do not have conscious control over the flow of your sexual energy, you can easily fall into the pattern which is probably most familiar to you—an exchange with one other person. In a triad, this means one person is left out. In a foursome, this means you have essentially two couples, not a foursome.

Even if everyone is happy with these configurations, you are missing an altogether different—and very powerful—dimension of merging on a group level. If you *do* find yourself involved in the synergy of group sex, you'll find that the complexity of multiple simultaneous exchanges is far beyond the capacity of the conscious mind. You will fall off the rising wave of energy once your thoughts begin to interfere. The bigger the wave, the farther and faster you will "wipe out."

Tantric knowledge is crucial to your success. Learning to open fully to sexual energies and to channel sexual energy consciously is critical in multipartner relationships, whether or not they involve group sex.

STEP 6: *LET JEALOUSY BE YOUR TEACHER*

Jealousy can lead you to the very places where you most need healing. It can be your guide into your own dark side and show you the way to total self-realization. Jealousy can teach you how to live in peace with yourself and with the whole world—*if* you let it.

Sexual jealousy in particular is much feared, inspiring powerful and compelling emotions. Many try to escape the need to confront this inner demon by building a monogamous fortress. But such an external strategy will, at best, only keep this dragon at bay. Rather than denying or killing it, jealousy needs to be transformed. Like all fears, jealousy is most readily cured by encountering it face to face. Of course, it is wise to prepare yourself before jumping in over your head. How you prepare will depend in part on your existing level of jealousy.

Some people are drawn to polyamory because they experience relatively little jealousy. Frequently they are able to identify and deal with the underlying individual emotions such as fear of loss, competition or sexual excitement which others lump together as one big scary mess. They also may have a lot of self-confidence or belong to a subculture which considers jealousy unacceptable. They may have already acquired the skills to analyze and rationally evaluate their fears. Or they may come from a background which rewarded sharing and unselfishness.

These people may have such strong and effective defenses that they mistakenly conclude they have no jealousy. Total freedom from jealousy does not come easily in this culture, which assumes jealousy to be inevitable. If you believe that jealousy isn't a problem for you, observe carefully to see if you are short-circuiting your reactions or explaining them instead of getting to the root of them. You need to become *more sensitive* to the part of you who sometimes feels jealous. It's also possible that you avoid exceeding your comfort zone by choosing partners who are more jealous than you are or to whom you are not fully attracted. If this is the case, you need to take more risks.

On the other hand, you may experience such intense jealousy that overcoming it is inconceivable. Such people may end up having illicit affairs rather than risking being open with a partner who would then also expect to have multiple lovers. But if you doubt your ability to successfully practice polyamory, you sentence yourself to a lovestyle based on lies and deceit. Ironically, such people are often tormented by jealousy anyway, as they suspect their partner of cheating or wanting to cheat on them.

If your jealousy is very intense, you can begin by working on some related issues before getting into situations where you're likely to feel jealous. The previous five steps should be a good start. Pay special attention to any early experiences of abandonment or loss of trust. Obviously you can't reconstruct your personality overnight, but you can transform your jealous feelings if you're willing to invest the time and energy. Allowing your jealous self to lead you inward without getting lost will shed light on your darkest secrets. How do you do it? In the next chapter, we'll be examining jealousy in greater depth and considering a number of strategies for letting jealousy be your teacher.

STEP 7: CHOOSE A SPIRITUAL PATH

Many polyamorous people find that they must essentially reject the whole ethical and moral framework in which they were raised in order to move beyond sex-negative conditioning. If simple rebellion is your only motive, you'll find polyamory far too demanding. But if you let iconoclastic sentiments serve as the stimulus for a spiritual search, you'll find yourself standing on solid ground.

Few people realize that choosing polyamory means that you're embarking on a spiritual path. Nevertheless, a strong spiritual focus is critical for your success. Spiritual training will aid you in remaining centered when emotional storms threaten to sink your polyamorous ship. It will keep you focused on cultivating your own inner harmony when you are tempted to get caught up in the external drama. It will help you respond with love and compassion instead of reacting with anger and blame. Most of all, it will encourage you to view your relationships as a means of becoming more conscious of who you really are.

Try exploring belief systems which are inherently positive about multiple relationships. Pre-Judeo-Christian, goddess oriented, tribal or neopagan religions, Unitarian, Course in Miracles inspired, or modern secular humanist philosophy are some possibilities. Seek out teachers in which ever religious or spiritual tradition you were raised with who advocate situational ethics or the need to update outmoded practices.

All genuine spiritual paths will take you "home," but they also emphasize different facets, and they take different routes. They may also have different ways of expressing universal laws. Learn to discriminate between political propaganda broadcast by some religions and the *living truth* underlying genuine spiritual traditions. Trust your intuition. Beware of gurus or preachers who advise celibacy or monogamy for their followers but who privately have affairs with students. Find a path which uses the senses which come easiest for you. For example, if you most trust your feelings, choose a heart path such as Christianity or Sufism. If your thinking is more reliable, consider Zen Buddhism. Martial Arts or tantra yoga may be most appropriate to the physically inclined.

Whatever path you choose, practice it faithfully, and let it guide you in your journey.

STEP 8: LOOK AT THE BIG PICTURE

The shift from enforced monogamy and the nuclear family to polyamory and intentional families or tribal communities can most easily be embraced if we see it in the context of a larger shift toward a more balanced, peaceful, and sustainable way of life.

Monogamous marriage as we know it today is based on patterns established in Biblical times governing men's ownership of women. In Biblical days the law prescribed that women be stoned to death for taking a lover, but men were allowed as many secondary wives or concubines as they could afford. For most of recorded history, the absolute authority of the husband over his wife has been taken for granted and male violence against disobedient wives has been considered natural and right.

Author Riane Eisler refers to this type of culture which legally and socially favors males and devalues women and children, relies upon fear and violence to enforce its values, exploits the Earth, encourages rigid hierarchies, condemns pleasure, and glorifies war and over-consumption as Dominator culture.[1] These seemingly disparate elements are in fact part and parcel of an integrated way of life.

Correspondingly, polyamory is part of an integrated way of life, which Eisler calls Partnership culture. Partnership culture is characterized by the celebration of life and pleasure, ecological awareness, respect for human rights and for all species, empathy, peaceful resolution of conflict, cooperation and sharing of resources, honoring our bodies, equality and social justice.

Working to shift your whole life in the direction of Partnership culture will support you in creating a polyamorous lovestyle on many different levels. On a personal level, it will take you out of the futile dominator cycle of powerless victim, angry controller, and self-sacrificing rescuer. On a social level, it will bring you into contact with others who share your appreciation for innovative relationship designs. On a cultural level, it gives you an opportunity to contribute to creating a more sustainable future by joining with others who are choosing to devote their time and energy to an important global movement.

Chapter 5

ᚢᚱ

JEALOUSY AS GATEKEEPER

*"The only way out of jealousy is through it.
We may have to let jealousy have its way with us and do
it's job of reorienting fundamental values. Its pain comes,
at least in part, from opening up to unexplored territory
and letting go of old familiar truths in the face of unknown
and threatening possibilities."*

Thomas Moore, *Care of the Soul*

How ironic that some people attempt to manage their jealousy by exchanging vows of lifelong sexual fidelity while others do the opposite and seek jealousy insurance by making sure they always have a spare lover in the wings! Both are bound to fail because ultimately the only real solution to jealousy is to raise your consciousness. And this is why jealousy can be such an incredible gift. For jealousy can only flourish when your mental and emotional state is one of separation and fear.

Spiritual teachers throughout the ages have agreed that our primary purpose as human beings is to learn unconditional love. Jealousy can be a potent reminder, a cosmic rap on the knuckles, letting us know that we're heading in the wrong direction, for jealousy is the opposite of love. If we recognize polyamory as a path for psychological and spiritual growth, then jealousy is gatekeeper on this path, for none can pass who refuse to confront this powerful force.

Jealousy will continue to teach us all along the way, letting us know whenever it arises, we have another lesson to learn.

NATURE VERSUS NURTURE

Most people are prone to jealousy because of a combination of acquired beliefs and genetically programmed reactions. People often argue about whether human beings are inevitably jealous as a result of our biological heritage or whether jealousy is learned through cultural conditioning and personal experiences. As usual, this issue turns out to more readily fit a "both/and" model than an "either/or" approach. Still, the nagging question remains: How much is nature and how much is nurture?

A more meaningful question might be: Is it possible to overcome jealousy and its destructive effects or does choosing polyamory mean dooming oneself to suffer from jealous feelings and melodramatic crises for a lifetime? Or perhaps: How does jealousy affect me and what can I do about it? For some, the underlying question is this: Must I feel ashamed of my jealous feelings or can I accept them as normal and natural?

My own belief is that while humans may have an innate territorial instinct as do other animals, we must *learn* to view our lovers as territory or possessions which can be owned like property and which we have a right to control. Some of us have even learned to regard jealousy as a sign of love and feel insecure and unloved in its absence. In other words, jealousy, like other emotions, has definite physiological roots, but the stimuli which trigger jealousy are almost entirely culturally determined. Interestingly enough, these jealousy provoking stimuli strike close to the heart of our culture's patriarchal patterning. If we are aware of these jealousy buttons, we can learn to navigate these dangerous waters without running aground, but this is no substitute for the "job of reorienting fundamental values" as Thomas Moore puts it.

Nearly everyone in our monogamous society learns early in life that lovers have exclusive rights. We are conditioned to believe that if our beloved is interested in someone else, we may be replaced. But this expectation of loss is learned, not hard wired, in both men and women. Imagine a culture in which your partner's attraction to another signified opportunities for greater pleasure and intimacy. Would jealousy occur in this context?

If we look at the behavior of our closest primate relatives, bonobo chimpanzees[1] we find that both males and females have numerous sex partners and this doesn't seem to create any conflict within the group. In fact, observers have noted that bonobos utilize sexual activity to facilitate group bonding and to defuse potential conflicts, for example, by sharing sexually prior to dividing up food.

Nevertheless, humans have such a long history of accepting sexual jealousy as inevitable that it's difficult to simply talk ourselves out of it. Just because a behavior is learned, doesn't mean that it's easy to change or that we chose to learn it or that we should feel ashamed that we've learned it. Still, by choosing a belief system which considers jealousy to be an inescapable part of our nature, we resign ourselves to allowing jealousy to control us. If instead we choose to believe that jealousy is learned, then surely we can unlearn it, opening up the possibility of freeing ourselves from its tyranny.

WHAT IS JEALOUSY?

Jealousy is one of the least studied of all human emotions. It does not even appear in the index of Daniel Goleman's groundbreaking book on emotional literacy, *Emotional Intelligence*.[2] Very little scientific data on jealousy exists and what there is deals mostly with the attitudes and thoughts associated with jealousy rather than with the emotion itself. Researchers seem to agree that on a cognitive behavioral level, jealousy is a reaction to a partner's real or imagined experience with a third party and that jealousy is more likely to occur in a person who is both dependent and insecure.[3] My own observation is that jealousy is most often found when a person's need for control is threatened.

Jealousy also has a spiritual dimension. In essence, jealousy indicates a crisis of faith. It is part of conditional love. If you will only love when you're assured of having your love returned, then you make yourself vulnerable to jealousy.[4] On a more practical level, we could say simply that jealousy is a message that your relationship needs work of some kind. It is certainly a very effective way of getting our attention!

What really interests me, however, is the actual physical experience of jealousy and the internal energetic events which create this experience. People commonly describe jealous sensations as gut wrenching, agitating, and overpoweringly unpleasant. While different people become jealous for different reasons, the actual feelings are remarkably consistent from person to person, though they may vary in intensity. Still, there is a dearth of information on this aspect of jealousy. I found I had to rely on examining my own inner process in order to develop some understanding of the internal sensations we call jealousy. I

invite you to do the same. Here's what I found to be true
for myself.

I am not vulnerable to jealousy unless I'm already feeling
both love and sexual arousal. Love opens the heart center
and creates a sense of unity, of connection with others.
Opening the sex center releases a high voltage energy flow
throughout the body and increases my connection to Earth.
Both love and sex are very pleasurable almost to the point of
being addictive. They increase my sensitivity to stimuli of all
kinds and at the same time raise my pain threshold.

If something then occurs which I perceive might separate
me from my beloved or love object, fear and anger arise
within me. The fear instructs my body to shut down the
free flow of energy, to constrict my sexual energy. The
anger closes my heart. But at the same time, my body is still
responding to the love and sexual arousal my beloved
inspires with the urge to open up. These contradictory
impulses bewilder the rational mind. It cannot gracefully
contain such duality. It labels this churning, open-and-close-
at-the-same-time sensation "jealousy" and strives to avoid it
at all costs.

JEALOUSY IS NOT BETRAYAL

Many people have jealousy confused with betrayal. In
jealousy the primary issue is fear of losing your love object.
This is scary enough for most people without mixing in the
reality of lies, withholds, and half truths. Feelings of betrayal
arise when *trust* has been shaken because of a perceived
deception or a breach of faith. Because so many people are
dishonest about their attraction to others or unilaterally
break monogamous agreements to have secret affairs,
jealousy and betrayal are often linked together.

One of my lovers felt betrayed as well as jealous of my attraction to another man even though we had a crystal clear agreement that we were each free to be polyamorous because on an emotional level he unconsciously believed that polyvalent love was unfaithful. If I really loved him, how could I also be open to someone else? His sense of betrayal turned out to be more difficult to resolve than the jealousy itself, which faded when it became obvious that I wasn't going to leave him for another man.

Conversely, Josh betrayed his lover, Amelia, by lying about his illicit affair with Catherine and then labeled Amelia's upset as jealousy rather than betrayal. When he then urged Amelia to get over her jealousy so that the couple could embark on an open relationship, he greatly impeded both the healing process and the transition to polyamory. In this case, his betrayal must be acknowledged and forgiven before it's appropriate to even consider working on the jealousy which might arise in a consensually open relationship.

TYPES OF JEALOUSY

One of most confusing things about jealousy is that each person's jealousy is not the same. Different people are triggered by different types of situations and have different kinds of reactions. Certain people are much more intensely affected than others. For this reason, some people feel that it's not useful to lump all these different experiences together and call them by one name.

I believe that recognizing and labeling jealousy as a single entity despite its many forms helps us to cope with it more effectively. However, it is definitely important to discover which types of jealousy are affecting you and your loved ones so that you can respond appropriately. The following

categories and their descriptions are based on those
identified by Ron Mazur.[5]

Possessive jealousy is much more common in
monogamous couples than among the intentionally
polyamorous for the simple reason that it is triggered by a
perceived threat to exclusive possession of the love object.
People who feel a need for exclusive possession are rarely
attracted to polyamory.   In this rather primitive type of
jealousy one's partner is regarded as property – private
property. Possessive jealousy occurs when a relationship is
characterized by commitment without trust. The message is
"You belong to me, and if I can't have you nobody can." This is the
type of jealousy most likely to lead to violent behavior where
in its most extreme form a jealous husband murders his
devoted wife because he suspects her of having another
lover.   Possessive jealousy was, until recently, implicitly
sanctioned by our society as evidenced by laws which did
not consider a man guilty of murder if he killed his wife or
her lover after finding them in bed together.

Exclusion jealousy frequently occurs in polyamory. The
issue here is not refusal to share a partner, but rather fear
that others are not going to share with you. Typically there
is a desire to be included at all times. Exclusion jealousy is
triggered when the jealous party feels that he or she is being
left out or deprived of equal time and attention.   The
message is *"How come you have all the fun?"* If the jealous party
is actually being neglected, perhaps because a new and
exciting lover has just come on the scene, exclusion jealousy
will be especially intense. Often this type of jealousy can be
managed by scheduling "date nights" when all partners see
outside lovers at the same time.

Competition jealousy is also quite common in polyamory. The primary problem here is that the jealous person begins to compare themselves with another lover and becomes convinced that he or she is inadequate in some way. The message here is *"You think I'm not good enough."* Competition jealousy is triggered in response to the fear that whatever made this relationship *special* is being shared with or surpassed by another. A person suffering from competition jealousy needs constant reassurance, but the relief is usually temporary. Sometimes competition jealousy can be managed by allowing the jealous person to create an "approved list" of non-threatening lovers for his or her partner to choose from.

Ego jealousy In ego jealousy the underlying issue is usually a concern about what others will think. This person may not be disturbed by sharing a lover as long as no one else knows about the situation, but is afraid others will judge him or her to be inadequate if it's know that their partner desires another lover. Sometimes ego jealousy arises out of fear of being seen as a cuckold. The message here is *"You've humiliated me."* The intensity of ego jealousy can be affected by timing, mood, or how you feel about a partner's lover. Unlike competition jealousy where the intensity of the jealousy will increase with the perceived desirability of the other lover, ego jealousy will be most intense when the other lover is seen as unworthy or disagreeable in some way.

Fear jealousy is probably the most basic type of jealousy, the one that most people anticipate when they contemplate polyamory. The basic issue here is the concern that your partner will leave you for someone else. Images of rejection, loneliness, and scarcity usually accompany the primary fear of loss. This type of jealousy whispers *"What if my lover finds someone else better?"* Of course it's obvious to the rational mind that your lover can just as easily fall in love with someone else if you have an agreement to be monogamous, but jealousy is rarely rational. Furthermore, the monogamous mindset dictates that he or she may well leave you if someone better shows up.

The unspoken assumption here is that engaging in sex makes falling in love more likely, and that falling in love with a new person means falling out of love with an existing partner. In fact, some people routinely operate this way, while others do not, irrespective of their identity as polyamorous or monogamous. Fear jealousy effectively reminds us that we've come to depend on a relationship for security, predictability, and self worth. It is best addressed by taking the time to feel one's own center and practicing being in the present moment rather than worrying about the past or the future.

WHAT TO DO IF YOU'RE FEELING JEALOUS

When jealousy taps you on the shoulder, your first response must always be to acknowledge it and to give thanks for this opportunity to grow. Remember that jealousy will illuminate your shadow, bringing your dark side to the forefront so you can get acquainted with the disowned, unloved fragments of personality which must be brought to consciousness before they can assume their proper place as part of an integrated whole. Don't waste precious energy trying to convince yourself that nothing's going on. Instead, learn to listen respectfully to the part of you who feels jealous without mistaking it for your whole self or allowing it to dictate your actions. This process is sometimes called *disidentification* or *voice dialogue* or *working with sub personalities*. Your goal here is simply to tune into your own feelings and find the source of your upset. Remind yourself that if you leap into action prematurely you may make matters worse. First, try to find out what your jealousy is showing you about yourself and your relationships with others by simply observing your own feelings and thoughts.

Second, seek support from your partner(s), friends, or an experienced therapist. Communicate as clearly as you can what you're experiencing and tell them what you would like from them without engaging in blame or making demands. If you need help in learning how to focus on your feelings without getting overwhelmed by them, this is *not* a good time to substitute friendly advice for professional help. However, a friend or lover can assist you by helping you *breathe through* your jealousy crisis.

We were already using the technique of circular breathing[6] in our *Love Without Limits* workshops to facilitate bonding and raise the group consciousness when we discovered that breathwork is a powerful tool for transforming jealousy! The only drawback is that many people resist using the breath to move through their jealousy because they're unwilling to let it go and give up the victim role they've taken on. If you really want results, try this. (If you have chronic health problems, recent surgery, heart disease, epilepsy or if you are pregnant consult your health care professional first.)

You will probably need someone to sit with you and remind you to keep breathing. Of course, a little empathy feels good too. Any nonjudgmental friend or lover will do, or you can seek out someone who has experience with some kind of breathwork or other healing modalities. Find a quiet place where you can make lots of noise but will be undisturbed for at least an hour, preferably two. Have plenty of warm blankets on hand since you may get cold.

Remove any belts, jewelry, or tight clothing. Begin by lying on your back and breathing in and out through the mouth with no pause in between the breaths. Find a comfortable rhythm which is a bit deeper and faster than your normal breath. Continue to breathe this way for at least an hour. Don't worry if you get dizzy or your hands or feet get tingly, numb, or cramped up. An hour may seem like a long time initially, but if you can continue breathing for the first ten minutes, the rest of the time will fly by.

Many people have a tendency to space out and forget to continue the circular breath. Tell your companion to instruct you to keep breathing deeper and faster or to breathe loudly near your ear whenever you return to your normal breath. You may also want to experiment with having your companion place a hand over your heart or your belly or your genitals while you breathe. Allow yourself to cry or make noises or move your body, but always return to the breath as soon as you can.

Each breathing session is different so be prepared for anything and everything to occur. You will probably gain some insights into your current situation, and it's very likely that when you return to your normal consciousness jealousy will have relaxed its grip at least temporarily. Use this opportunity to share your experience with your partner and see if there's anything you've been keeping secret or were unaware of that you need to express.

One message that jealousy always brings is to remember to love yourself! Go beyond liking yourself or appreciating yourself, and shower yourself with love. Take time to nurture yourself. Treat yourself to a massage, a gift, or a visit to your favorite place. Take some time out for whatever brings you pleasure.

WHAT TO DO IF YOUR PARTNER IS FEELING JEALOUS

The first thing you must do if your partner is jealous is to assess the potential for violence. If your partner has a history of violent behavior or has made threats to harm you, you need to protect yourself. Jealous rage can be lethal so remove yourself from the situation if you have any concerns about your safety. Hopefully, no drastic measures will be necessary, but if you cannot rely on your partner's self control, it's too big a risk to invite jealousy to be your teacher.

Next, let your partner know you're there for him or her. Make yourself available to listen while they express their hurt. Try to validate their experience, for example by saying that you understand how they feel, even if you don't agree with everything they say. Be generous with hugs, encouragement, and affection. If your partner is sincerely asking jealousy to teach them, let them know they have your full support. Honor their courage.

At the same time, let your partner know that you will not be manipulated by their jealousy. If they're blaming you or being verbally abusive, try not to react by slinging a few stones of your own. Instead, respond by letting them know that their behavior is not acceptable to you and is creating more distance between you. If you're having trouble communicating in a loving way, suggest calling in a neutral friend or a therapist.

Next take a look inside yourself. Is your partner acting out your own unexpressed jealousy? Are you carelessly pushing your partner's jealousy buttons? Are you neglecting to let your partner know that you love and value him or her? Are you taking your partner for granted?   If you continually attract highly jealous partners, you need to ask yourself why. What goodies do you get out of having a jealous partner? Does your partner's jealousy make you feel powerful? Desirable? Secure? Do you enjoy having the upper hand? Take this opportunity to let your partner's jealousy teach you too.   If you discover that you had a part in creating the jealousy crisis, own up to it.

MANAGING JEALOUSY

Thus far we've been talking about ways to transform jealousy into a valuable teacher and move through it. Sometimes it's more appropriate, or at least easier, to sidestep jealousy and avoid the turmoil it brings. This may be necessary to bring the intensity down to a level where you can approach it more fruitfully.   Or you may choose to wait for a more suitable time to confront jealousy head on.   The danger here is that if you continue to manage jealousy instead of embracing it, you may limit your own growth and find yourself adapting to a disempowering situation. Use the following strategies for jealousy management with discretion.

Negotiation can work wonders in preventing jealousy from disrupting your life. If you and your partner(s) are able to identify your jealousy triggers, you can find ways to work around them. If you've already taken the time to observe yourself and know which people or circumstances push your jealousy buttons, you can ask your partner to experiment with more palatable alternatives.

Evelyn and Daniel discussed polyamory on their first date and were delighted to find that neither one of them was interested in monogamy. But after their marriage a year later Evelyn found herself feeling possessive.   When Julia displayed attraction for Daniel, Evelyn quickly found herself feeling jealous. But when Julia invited Evelyn to have lunch with her and asked Evelyn's permission to date Daniel, Evelyn found that her jealousy nearly disappeared, and she readily consented. Realizing that she needed to be asked for permission in order to feel comfortable, Evelyn asked Daniel to instruct any women he wanted to date to ask her permission first. Daniel was happy to find such a simple means to manage Evelyn's jealousy and willingly complied with her request.

Patrick's jealousy was not so easily handled. When he and Karen decided to embark on an open relationship, he found that while he enjoyed his freedom to be with other women, he couldn't stand the thought of Karen making love with another man who might take her away from him. Patrick asked Karen to agree that they would only date married couples since he felt safer with men who were already committed to another woman. Karen was willing to try this for one year if Patrick would agree to work on his jealousy during that time.

Patrick began by using *systematic desensitization* to reduce his emotional reactivity. First he constructed a detailed list of jealousy-arousing experiences, ordered from the least threatening to the most threatening. With Karen's support he chose a time when they were feeling relaxed and confident to try imagining the least uncomfortable scenario, which for him was a double date with another couple. Patrick was able to stay relaxed and free of jealousy until he began to imagine that after dinner and dancing the two couples returned home and Karen went into their bedroom with the other man, leaving Patrick in the living room with the other woman. He had gone too far too fast and needed to take smaller steps.

Next time, he changed the scenario so that both couples went into the bedroom and made love side by side with their own partners. Then they all snuggled up together. This time Patrick felt only a twinge of jealousy. Gradually over several desensitization sessions he adjusted his fantasy to increase the amount of contact Karen had with the other man. Then he imagined Karen and the other man getting up and going to the living room, leaving Patrick alone with the other woman. This scenario felt so comfortable it gave Patrick enough confidence to go back to his original fantasy of Karen going into their bedroom with the other man after a double date. Again his jealousy flared up.

I suggested that Patrick try out another location, such as a two room suite in a hotel. This worked much better for him. In fact, Patrick was able to imagine Karen spending the rest of the night with the other man in their hotel suite without feeling much jealousy. It appeared that he had inadvertently hit one of his own jealousy buttons by imagining Karen in their own "special" bed with another man.

Some months later Patrick and Karen met a couple they both liked and were able to develop a warm friendship which slowly became sexual. Patrick remained jealousy free until Karen told him she wanted to go away for the weekend with the other man. He again implemented the systematic desensitization technique and after several weeks of work felt he was ready to spend the weekend without Karen.

Jealousy was his constant companion but by now he was able to start letting jealousy be his teacher without panicking. Since he had developed a trusting relationship with the other couple, he was able to share his fears with them as well as with Karen and to accept their support.

COMPERSION

Compersion is a term invented by the now defunct Kerista Community to describe an emotion which is the opposite of jealousy. We say that we are feeling compersion when we take delight in a beloved's love for another. Compersion tends to be especially strong when we find that two people we love feel affection for each other.

If you've ever experienced this sensation, I'm sure you know exactly what I'm talking about although you may not have had a word to identify your feelings. If you can't imagine feeling compersion instead of jealousy, you might begin to move in this direction by focusing on the happiness your beloved feels at the prospect of an additional loving relationship rather than your own discomfort about the possibility of losing someone very precious to you. Just having a concept which acknowledges that you have the potential of feeling joy and expansion rather than fear and contraction in response to a loved one's sharing their love with others can go a long way toward transforming jealousy.

Chapter 6

CR

MAKING THE TRANSITION TO POLYAMOROUS RELATING

"Your love is located within you. It is yours to nurture and savor, to give to others in any way you choose. Love must be without qualifications or demands. You must learn to find ecstasy in other people's happiness. Once you feel love for yourself, it is quite normal to give it away."
Wayne Dyer, *Gifts from Eykis*

Some people repress their desire for polyamory, because they're afraid no one will marry them if they admit the truth. Many more become aware of their desire for polyamory only after having already made a commitment to be monogamous. Often they act on this desire without first thinking through their options and the respective consequences. This mirrors our cultural preference for short-term fixes without regard to long-term results.

Others remain single, carefully avoiding any long-term commitment because, consciously or unconsciously, they are unwilling to risk trapping themselves in a monogamous relationship. Some have been monogamously married before and know that it isn't for them. Often such a person will tell themselves (and their lovers) that they are looking for a mate, but they just don't seem to be able to find the right person. If a relationship starts feeling really good, they will usually break it off—or take on a new lover.

Both groups may find that polyamory offers them a way to build stable relationships without giving up too much of their freedom. But whichever group you are a member of, you have to be willing to make some *major* changes.

IF YOU'RE SINGLE

The transition to polyamory for a single person is relatively simple. In this case, you can make the shift with no broken promises and no broken hearts.

Let any current lovers know that you are not monogamous and that you don't plan to commit to monogamy while clearly expressing your intentions for this relationship. Do you see this person as a potential mate, a sexual friend, or a temporary lover? Do you love him/her? Do you have any major reservations about getting closer? Are you open and available for whatever develops between you? Be prepared to explain the precepts of polyamorous relating and new paradigm relationships and to fully disclose any relevant personal sexual history. If you know what kind of lovestyle you ultimately want to create, be sure to discuss that, too.

However, you needn't present your position with mono-choice rigidity either. After all, who knows what the future will bring? Just make it obvious that you're unwilling to automatically go along with someone else's expectations or with society's monogamous program. As one conscious polyamorous man told his new lover, "It's my penis, and I'll decide what I want to do with it."

Some of your lovers will appreciate your clear communication, while others may quickly conclude that your relationship is over. But don't let this deter you. You'll never find what you're looking for if you keep yourself entangled with partners who are single mindedly pursuing monogamy.

Be sure to repeat this process with each new person you date. It needn't come up in the first five minutes of conversation, as in "Hi, my name is Dana and I'm into polyamory. Do you know what that is?" But if you are interested enough to get together more than a couple of times, and *definitely before becoming sexual,* you should acknowledge your preference for polyamory.

This kind of disclosure can cut down on your sexual adventures but, if you want to find partners who can share the joys of polyamory with you, it will benefit you in the long run.

IF YOU'VE ALREADY BROKEN A MONOGAMOUS COMMITMENT

If you have already violated an agreement to be monogamous, and you cannot honestly say that it will never happen again, it's still not too late to start acting responsibly. Come out to your partner. It's possible that your partner will choose to end the relationship rather than make the transition to polyamory, but this is a risk you will have to take. Of course, this is assuming that *your* choice is to stay with your current partner.

If you are using illicit affairs as a message to your partner that you want out of the relationship, save everyone a lot of misery and find the courage to tell him or her that you want to separate. If you are checking out new potential partners before letting go of your current one, find a psychotherapist to help you overcome your fear of being alone. Don't use your partner as a security blanket. If you get your thrills from seeing how many illicit affairs you can get away with, consider joining a twelve step group for sex addicts. But if you want to stay with your current partner in some kind of consensual polyamorous relationship, you can begin by letting him or her *exercise the right to make an informed decision.*

Hopefully, the decision to come out will ultimately reflect the depth of your love for each other and the general quality of your relationship. Still, some people simply do not have enough self-esteem or are not open-minded enough to *even consider the possibility* of a nontraditional love relationship. Some people have such strong feelings about the total wrongness of polyamory that they will find it impossible to be objective about the subject, especially once their trust has been violated. Don't underestimate your partner, but if you're pretty sure your partner will object to polyamory, you may be better off acknowledging that you are mismatched from the start and prepare to be rejected. In any case, your monogamous relationship will have to "die" in some sense before it can be reborn in a new form. As in any grieving process, you can expect to encounter some strong emotions.

It's very likely that your partner will rant and rave or cry and moan and vigorously express hurt and anger when you inform him or her about your infidelity. In fact, you should be concerned if you don't get much of a response, because it probably means that your partner is going to have a hard time getting to a place where she or he can forgive you. However, if you suspect that one or both of you may become physically violent, it's a good idea to choose a time and location with some built-in controls. A restaurant, a willing friend's home, or a public park near a police station can all offer some incentives for good behavior.

Give your partner plenty of time to digest the information before you discuss what comes next. Make sure your partner knows that you love him or her and that you want to continue the relationship. Invite your partner to attend a *Love Without Limits* workshop so they can learn more about polyamorous lovestyles and the people who are choosing them. Many people will need to stay angry for days, weeks or even months. Some will "pay you back" by having an affair of their own. You may find that you can get through this stage more quickly by agreeing to be strictly monogamous at least until you've decided what your next steps will be in this relationship.

If your partner is still too angry to talk intimately and openly after a couple of months, or if either of you have not yet developed this ability, you're going to need professional help. Look for a counselor who is experienced in working with polyamorous couples. Any skilled and truly open-minded therapist will be adequate but beware—the cultural conditioning is very strong, and the therapist's *own* prejudices may interfere.

THE TURNING POINT

Some couples are fortunate enough to move on to the next stage where the focus is on becoming defenselessly open with each other as you try to create a new relationship based on the expression of truth coupled with a trusting respect that serves to deepen the intimacy. Don't rush it! Hopefully, one or both of you will have by now given up your habit of clinging to the relationship at all costs. When you reach the point of being guided by the truth more than by your fear of rejection, you will know you are on the right road. Again, if you need help, find it! Many excellent relationships seminars are available. Attending a *Love*

Without Limits weekend workshop can give you the opportunity to talk with others who are grappling with these issues, in one form or another, can give you the courage you need to transform your relationship.

Anything can happen now that you've begun to share more of yourselves with each other. You may even find that additional partners are less appealing to you now that your existing relationship has become more exciting. But if you're unwilling to *re*commit to lifelong monogamy, don't lose sight of that as you begin to re-negotiate the terms of your marriage.

RE-NEGOTIATION

One thing you will want to do when you reach the stage of re-negotiation is to ask your partner to try to understand the appeal that polyamory has for you. This is not the same thing as asking your partner to *agree* to polyamory. Rather, *it is a request for understanding.* Books like this one, or perhaps some science fiction or Robert Rimmer novels dealing with multi-partner relating may help give him or her a new perspective on the subject.

Your partner's anxiety can be reduced by knowing what specific needs and desires you are trying to meet with additional lovers. If more or different sex is involved, this may be the perfect time to work on enhancing your sexual connection. It's important to do this anyway, before expanding your relationship. On the other hand, if you have needs your partner can't possibly meet alone, i. e. you're bisexual or you want to have group sex or you want more frequent sex than your partner wants, she or he may be relieved to know that she or he has not failed you. And he or she may be willing to try incorporating your needs on a fantasy level while you're in the process of exploring the next steps.

Another important area to address is your partner's specific fears and objections to polyamory. Often people are afraid that their partner will find someone else they like better and leave. Point out that this may actually be more likely in a monogamous relationship because in polyamory you can find someone else you like and stay. It requires a major shift in thinking—and feeling—to realize that "trading up" is a very alien concept in polyamory. In polyamory the vision is to add partners, not subtract them. Emphasizing very inclusive forms of polyamory where individual "dates" are rare may help get this idea across. For example, you could agree that, until your partner is more comfortable with the idea of multiple partners, you will *both* participate in any phone calls, dinners or sex play that take place with other partners. If you are offering your partner this kind of control as a temporary measure, be sure to clearly spell out the time frame or other limiting factors in advance.

Often, getting to know and trust another potential lover will eliminate fears that she or he might steal your mate. Or it might turn up evidence that a new flame doesn't respect your existing commitment and, consequently, is not a suitable partner for an inclusive relationship. But logic is no match for early traumatic experiences. If either of you has a history of abandonment, you will need to do some healing in this area. Let your partner know that you will support and cooperate with any efforts he or she makes to overcome wounds to his or her psyche.

In general, a solid relationship will become stronger as a result of exploring new relationships. If your existing partnership is shaky, polyamory will quickly bring its weak points to the surface. This phenomenon may make it look like polyamory is the culprit, and it may seem to justify a reluctant partner's advocacy of monogamy. In truth, you are in no position to practice polyamory if your primary partnership is weak, but if it helps you identify new problem areas, polyamory has given you a valuable gift. Now that you're aware of the trouble spots in your relationship you can work on them. Sometimes you may even find that the best solution is to separate, but try to be clear about the underlying problems, rather than blaming everything on the monogamy/polyamory conflict.

Sometimes, the stumbling block can be summed up in one word: jealousy. Chances are that you, too, will experience some jealousy if your partner agrees to practice polyamory, so you may as well set a good example by demonstrating your willingness to work on your own jealousy first.

Some people experience such intense jealousy that it's inconceivable to them that they could ever overcome it. Others have relatively low levels of jealousy which may lead them to erroneously conclude that they have nothing to work on. Even though this emotion needs to be acknowledged, most people choose to avoid the admission that jealousy exists. But *jealousy can be a wonderful teacher.* If you are open to it, it will show you the way to inner peace and serenity, not to mention true love. With patience and caring, many people can free themselves from the tyranny of jealousy.

The mix of emotions generated by sharing a sexual partner are similar in many ways to the emotions generated by parenting children. Rage, frustration, feeling out of control, pushed beyond your limits, isolated—all of these are encountered at some time by every parent. Yet few people decide against having children because they're afraid they can't handle it. Some, especially those with a history of abuse, do decide to remain childless while others decide to put their energy elsewhere. But the majority manage somehow and almost always learn a great deal about themselves in the process. In the end, most people agree that raising children is one of the more gratifying parts of being human. Overcoming jealousy and sharing lovers can provide a similar challenge.

Whatever your partner's concerns, it's essential to listen carefully and sort out whether they are "show stoppers" or opportunities for deepening your relationship. That is, do they reflect basic value differences or are they pointers to solvable problems? If your partner's objections center around time and energy, and this is not a smoke screen for hidden emotional issues, it may be difficult to find solutions without undertaking a major lifestyle change. If you both have demanding careers or active hobbies or are parenting young children, it could be that you simply don't have time in your lives to develop more intimate relationships. In this case, you might agree to wait until the children are older. Or you could reduce your expenses and find part-time work, or plan an early retirement.

The reality is that polyamory does require extra time, especially in the beginning, and if you have too many other priorities and limited time, it's not an appropriate choice.

On the other hand, once you have established some form of stable inclusive relationship, you may find that you have more time and energy available because of the synergy released by your close association with others of like mind. As with so many issues, it's often a matter of choosing the right time to include others into your relationship. To successfully practice polyamory, your existing relationship must already be very satisfying for each of you. Devoting sufficient time and energy to enjoying each other *before* contemplating other partners is essential. If either of you fails to communicate fully and deeply so that you grow together, you will more than likely grow apart.

IF YOUR PARTNER HAS BROKEN
A MONOGAMOUS COMMITMENT

If your partner has been unfaithful, your first reaction is probably hurt, anger and a sense of betrayal. Your trust has been violated and amends must be made. Most people believe that, if the infidelity can be forgiven at all, the guilty party must promise never again to deviate from monogamy. For some people this is the only acceptable solution. But depending upon the circumstances and motivations involved, an agreement to practice polyamory can also ensure that your partner will never again violate the trust and commitment you have to each other.

Roger and Elizabeth had been unaware that each had a different understanding of the ground rules of their relationship. Because they had never discussed and clearly agreed to be either monogamous or polyamorous, Roger assumed that it was okay to fool around, and Elizabeth assumed that it wasn't. They weren't really sure what was acceptable to each other and what was not, and they were afraid to find out because more information might lead to conflict in their relationship or end it totally. In situations like these, an affair can be a catalyst for better communication and greater intimacy. Neither Roger nor Elizabeth, it turned out, was really opposed to polyamory, they had simply failed to consciously make a choice. When presented with some specific options, they found reaching an agreement relatively easy.

Peter and Carolyn did have an ironclad commitment to monogamy. When Peter confessed that he'd had an affair, they took the opportunity to look more closely at what they really wanted from each other. It turned out that it was not necessarily monogamy, per se, but fidelity and sensitivity to each other's feelings. No one wants to be deceived, misled or belittled by their beloved, but monogamy is not the only way to ensure that your partner will treat you with the total love, consideration and respect you expect and deserve! Peter had chosen a clumsy and unskilled way to let Carolyn know that he had problems with monogamy, but since there were no other serious problems in their relationship, they were able to create a more enduring relationship that better met both of their needs. Peter and Carolyn were wise enough to realize that human beings are not always monogamous by nature. By designing a relationship which took this into account instead of indulging in blame and guilt, they succeeded in preserving the intimacy and love they'd established with each other.

Sometimes, what it comes down to is this: Who or what do you love more? Your partner or your concept of an ideal relationship? What do you value more? Your happiness or your belief system? If your partner is willing to integrate other sexual partners in a way which doesn't detract from his or her relationship with you (see Chapter 2 for specifics) and to extend the same privileges to you, polyamory may work for you.

Of course, polyamory is not an appropriate choice for everyone. Don't agree to it just to please your partner. But don't rule it out either just because you've never considered it.

IF YOU'RE KEEPING A COMMITMENT TO
MONOGAMY YOU WISH YOU HADN'T MADE

Your route to polyamory can be smoother than the one we've just outlined. Your biggest problem may be getting your partner to take you seriously. You will also have to decide whether you're willing to continue being monogamous indefinitely, if that's what your partner wants, or whether you're willing to end the relationship if she or he continues to insist on monogamy.

One possibility is to suggest that *your partner be released from monogamy on a trial basis while you remain monogamous,* so she or he can investigate polyamory first hand without worrying about your escapades. Another is to agree that you both have veto power over any specific person or occasion. That is, you can make space in your relationship to share your polyamorous feelings with your partner while assuring him or her that you won't act on them without his or her permission. This is a way of honoring your commitment to be monogamous without withholding an important part of yourself. If your partner is very jealous, you may think it's a pretty stupid idea to risk his or her wrath for "nothing." But if there's to be any hope for a satisfying, intimate relationship, you're going to have to tell the truth and find ways to deal with the results.

You can begin by letting your partner know of your interest in polyamory. If you've already done this, it's probably time to let him or her know that you're ready for action. Timing is important. Find a time when you're both relaxed and free from any unusual stressors. Birthdays, anniversaries, pregnancy, new parenthood and just after love making are *not* good times.

By choosing to openly discuss your situation with your partner without breaking your commitment to him or her, you demonstrate your trustworthiness. Your partner may still be too angry to give you the credit you deserve for being honest; but if you make it clear that your ultimate goal is to increase the intimacy between you, you can immediately enter the *turning point* stage described above.

A TRUE STORY

If you think all this talk about being honest and getting what you want is pure fantasy, consider the following true story.

Mary and Doug had been married for eight years. She had carried on long-term and short-term affairs with both men and women for seven of these years. They both traveled extensively for their work and had no children, so it was easy for Mary to keep her varied sex life a secret from Doug. The logistics were easy, but Mary was tormented by the lack of integrity her lovestyle entailed. She loved Doug and valued their relationship, but her sex drive was much stronger than his—and she had a strong need for sexual intimacy with other women.

Early in their relationship, Doug had made it clear that he wanted a monogamous relationship. Mary had opted to try to conform to his wishes, although she knew from the start that polyamory felt more natural to her. After a year, she tried to renegotiate the agreement, but Doug wouldn't hear of it, so she began her clandestine affairs.

Finally, at the urging of her therapist and one of her lovers, she made a full confession to Doug, completely expecting him to divorce her. Doug was predictably furious and decided to move out. But Mary and her lover were both surprised when, after several months of separation, Doug decided that his love for Mary was greater than his attachment to monogamy. He was eager to hear about the possibilities for polyamory, and he and Mary quickly decided that they would explore this new territory together.

Within six months Doug was fully convinced that polyamory made a lot of sense, and Mary and Doug were more devoted to each other than ever. They tried a relationship with another couple which didn't work out, and Mary stopped seeing her other lovers because they weren't comfortable spending time with Doug. Both of them realized it would take a lot of effort to find other compatible partners and were relieved that they could tackle this dilemma together.

☃

COMING OUT POLY

"One of the commonest perversions of love is the effort to limit it to the private sphere. The Greeks had a special name for those apolitical persons who thought eros was appropriately expressed only in privacy. They were called 'idiot.' In its original sense, idiot signified a purely private person."

Sam Keen, *The Passionate Life*

The term *coming out* has been popularized by its use in the gay, lesbian and bisexual communities to describe the process of telling the truth about oneself and one's sexuality. Someone who has not yet *come out* is said to be *in the closet.* These concepts apply quite well to people with a *polyamorous (or poly) relationship orientation.* However, as we shall see, there are significant differences as well as significant parallels with the homosexual and bisexual experiences.

COMING OUT IS A PROCESS

Coming out is an ongoing process which occurs gradually over many years. It includes first *admitting to yourself* that you really are the way you are—in this case, admitting that you want to have more than one lover at time. Once you've recognized yourself as not being monogamous, you then have to sort out what you *do* want and learn to accept and to love yourself as you are. Part of coming out to yourself involves finding a label, name or description for your new identity.

You might think that accepting your polyamorous nature would be a simple matter, but most us of have been thoroughly indoctrinated to believe that we should be monogamous.   We're likely to expend energy trying to squeeze ourselves into a monogamous mold instead of considering the possibility that it's really okay to relate to more than one person at a time.

The first important step is to begin *letting other people know* about your polyamorous self.   Often the first people who are told are people whom you know will support, accept or at least not care very much about your sexual orientation. Usually the last people you're ready to come out to are the people who count the most—lovers, employers, parents and family.

Finally, you may feel that you needn't keep any secrets from anyone.   While you will continue to encounter new situations where you will be faced with decisions about how to present yourself, you will no longer be afraid of being discovered.

Polyamorous people are perhaps the last sexual minority to come out of hiding.   In an age when homosexuals demand church weddings and some cities have passed domestic partners ordinances which extend spousal privileges to same sex or unmarried couples, polyamory is still so socially unacceptable that we don't even have a widely understood *name* for it. This may be because variations in relationship orientation are perceived as even more of a threat to the established social order than variations in sexual orientation.

WHO IS POLY?

For the rest of this chapter we will use the word *poly* to refer to the relationship orientation of people who love and want to be intimate with more than one person at a time. This includes people who limit their sexual encounters to one person at a time while maintaining more than one ongoing relationship as well as people who want to engage in group sex with their partners. It excludes people who are only interested in indiscriminate, recreational sex in the absence of more holistic relating since sexual behavior alone does not define relationship orientation.

There is a wide variety of lovestyles among people who are inclined toward same-sex partners, with some choosing monogamy, others preferring to have only anonymous encounters and still others opting for multiple committed relationships. Those with a poly orientation are also very diverse. They may be gay, straight or bisexual, and they cover the entire middle ground between monogamy and promiscuity.

If we include in this group everyone who's had two sexualoving partners during the same time period, we're talking about a lot of people. If we include people who constantly fantasize about other partners but don't act out their desires for fear of destroying their monogamous marriage, we're talking about a lot of people, so many that we can hardly call it a minority group! Even if we only include people who have habitually had more than one lover at a time, whether single or married, there are a lot of polys out there. But it's hard to know exactly how many.

THE FALSE DICHOTOMY

People's sexual and relationship orientations don't always fit neatly into separate categories. For example, when I was in graduate school studying sexology, I was taught that on the homosexual-heterosexual dimension there really isn't a dichotomy, rather there is a continuum. That is, on a scale of 1 to 10 where 1 is 100% heterosexual and 10 is 100% homosexual, most people will be somewhere in between the two extremes. People who are "somewhere in between" may—or may not—identify themselves as *bi*sexual. Until recently, most did not. I didn't think of myself as bisexual at the time even though it was clear to me when presented with the continuum concept that I fit somewhere in the middle.

To complicate matters even more, some people insist that there's no such thing as a stable bisexual identity, that people who think they're bisexual are really in transition from one extreme to the other. Only recently have relatively large numbers of self-identified bisexuals come forward saying, "Gender is not the most important factor in who I love or don't love, and I consider myself to be bisexual whether I happen to be with a same sex partner or opposite sex partner at any given time." Bisexuals often remind us that our sexuality is more fluid than we like to think, that we all have the potential to love people of both genders.

Monogamy and promiscuity may also be more of a continuum than a dichotomy. Hardly anyone has only one sexual partner for their whole lifetime, and hardly anyone has never had an exclusive relationship for at least a brief period. Most of us are somewhere in between. And while some of those who are in between *are* in transition, others find that having more than one committed sexualove relationship at a time is what feels most right to them. This does not preclude choosing to be with only one partner for a period of time, it just means that there's no expectation that the relationship will remain forever monogamous. Sometimes this in-between-group doesn't identify as poly simply because they've never met or even heard of a person who has come out poly. This was certainly the case with me, even though I had a long history of being drawn to multiple partners.

There's another strange thing about our efforts to categorize ourselves and others. Not only do we try to make an *either/or* choice where a *both/and* choice makes more sense, but we tend to put ourselves at the most desirable pole and to put others at the less desirable pole even though many of us are in the middle. This phenomenon is most obvious when we look at racial or ethnic identities. A person whose mother is white and whose father is black will be considered black in our culture. In Nazi Germany, a person with even a trace of Jewish blood was considered Jewish. However, many people of mixed blood "pass" as members of the dominant culture.

Similarly, serial monogamists, who might more accurately be called serial polygamists, pass as monogamists both to themselves and to society at large. And committed polys may reject the poly label because of its negative association with promiscuity in our culture. With models for responsible multipartner relationships largely invisible, the concept of nonmonogamy is usually seen as a male scam to avoid commitment or as evidence of nymphomania in a woman. Who would want to identify themselves with either of those?

WHERE HAVE ALL THE POLYS GONE?

If there are so many of us, how come we're so invisible? One reason is that so many of us have not come out—even to ourselves. The concepts of coming out and being in the closet exist in the first place because a homosexual can easily present a public appearance of heterosexuality and go undetected unless she or he *chooses* to reveal him or herself. However, in order to have a sexual encounter, a homosexual must come out at least to his or her prospective partner. In fact, the term *coming out* was originally used to refer to a first time same sex experience.

Someone who is poly, however, *can have sexual encounters without coming out to his or her partners* as long as group sex is not involved. And the vast majority of polys rarely if ever engage in group sex. The polysexual is in somewhat the same situation as the bisexual who can, if she or he chooses, pass as straight with an opposite sex lover and pass as gay or lesbian with a same sex lover. And it is no coincidence that, until the last few years, bisexuals have been pretty much invisible in both the heterosexual and homosexual worlds. Sadly, one of the greatest fears that bisexuals have about coming out is that it will be assumed that they're *not monogamous!*

Because polys can remain safely hidden while satisfying many sexual and emotional needs, you may lack the motivation to disclose your polyamorous feelings. It's even possible to avoid coming out to yourself, by telling yourself that you're trying to choose between several partners. It's not that you *want* more than one lover, you're just having a hard time making up your mind—a very hard time. Or you may tell yourself that you don't really care for one of your partners, you're just there out of habit or obligation.

It's natural to be reluctant to admit to yourself and others that what you want is something that's widely held to be immoral and indecent—not to mention impossible! But trying to repress, lie about, rationalize or otherwise deny your polyamorous nature can be very damaging to yourself, your loved ones and your fellow polys.

THE PRICE WE PAY FOR STAYING IN THE CLOSET

To go through life with the sense that one is guarding a dirty—and possibly dangerous—little secret is to go through life with an ever-present feeling of isolation, alienation and disharmony. Even if you limit your polysexuality to the realm of fantasy and desire, you may experience a troubling sensation of not quite fitting in, or being different from others in some mysterious, unknown way. The closeted person often feels as though he or she is from another planet. Depression, low self-esteem and a lack of spontaneity are frequently problems.

It's hard to find compatible, like-minded partners if you can't be up front about who you are and what you want. Many people are reluctant to risk alienating precious friends by confessing their interest in polyamorous relating. Others are understandably fearful of triggering a jealousy attack if they were to honestly express their attraction to a neighbor's spouse. Often, it ends up feeling safer to seek out partners among strangers who have already declared themselves to be polyamorous.

But with so many polys in the closet, it can be hard to find compatible partners even in a context where everyone is willing to let others know that they're open to a polyamorous lovestyle. As with any suspect subculture, the people most likely to come out initially include those who are already so far out of the mainstream they have little to lose by revealing themselves. This further distorts the already bizarre picture the public has of us, as well as flooding an already small "gene pool" with potential partners who are unsuitable for the average poly. Then there are people who are still in the early stages of coming out to themselves and who will waffle and run when faced with the prospect of an actual polyamorous relationship.

The dearth of out-of-the-closet role models for creating a stable, legitimate poly lovestyle combined with limited access to potential partners can create an atmosphere of pessimism, stuckness and scarcity. Whether you have come out or not, you may doubt that a healthy poly lovestyle is really a possibility. You may have difficulty finding the kinds of experiences which would help you to grow in the direction you've chosen. You may give up and make a monogamous commitment out of frustration rather than conviction.

Miraculously, some people find that they've established satisfying polyamorous relationships despite the lack of social support. While they are comfortably "out" to themselves and their partners, they still feel that they must hide their lovestyle from neighbors, employers, friends and extended family. They may disguise a primary partner as a "roommate" or "housekeeper." They may camouflage a secondary partner as a "business associate" or "friend of the family." They may avoid restaurants and theatres where someone might recognize them. They may simply keep quiet about their unconventional secret. These people may be less troubled than their solitary closet dwellers because they have each other for company. But they too pay a price for hiding out, and often feel isolated and afraid of being discovered.

Those who are actively nonmonogamous without coming out to their lovers, spouses and children, may hide their pain and feelings of worthlessness under the excitement of intrigue and illicit adventure.   But one lie—or omission—leads to another, and pretty soon you're lying all of the time. Leading a double life can be stressful as well as effectively limiting deep intimacy with others. When you're found out, you not only hurt the ones you love, you condition your partners to associate nonmonogamy with the betrayal of trust, a confusion from which they may never recover.

By adding your weight to the legacy of deceit and infidelity that polys everywhere must contend with, you strengthen the bad reputation which may have led you—and others—to stay in the closet in the first place.   So we are all disempowered by each other's cowardice, just as we can all be empowered by each other's courage.

THE REWARDS OF COMING OUT

One of the best gifts you can give yourself is the *permission to be who you are.*   By loving yourself unconditionally and respecting all of your qualities and inclinations, *you allow yourself to be at peace.* This is a gift to us all.

Permission to *be* who you are doesn't mean giving yourself license to *do* anything at all, as people sometimes fear. Rather it is a way to become more conscious about what you want and why, and so become better equipped to find a balance between pleasing only yourself and pleasing everyone but yourself.

For some people, coming out poly can be a very natural step which doesn't involve any additional lifestyle changes. You may have already created a life with which polyamory can harmoniously blend. There is no need to separate yourself from monogamous friends and associates or to over emphasize your differences. There is no need to become obsessed with creating polyamorous relationships. Regardless of your situation, it is the internal act of acknowledging who you are which will prove to be most transformational.

Accepting yourself as a polyamorous person is an important part of the larger process of self-differentiation and integration. It liberates you from having to hide an important part of yourself; hiding tends to slow down or even stop the whole growth process. Worse yet, when we deny our poly nature, we tend to project it outside ourselves and see sex-crazed demons under every rock which we then try to restrain and control. Or we unconsciously transform our unused sexualoving potential into hatred and aggression. What a different world this would be if we were all psychologically whole and complete!

Coming to terms with your relationship orientation is an essential—and often neglected—part of growing up and becoming a mature human being. Not only does it contribute to your personal well-being, it increases your capacity to share intimacy with others. Coming out makes it *possible* to establish ethical and stable multipartner relationships. It allows you to be more open and honest with everyone you know, because you no longer have to censor yourself to prevent an inadvertent slip.

By coming out you not only transform your own life, you help transform the entire culture. Each person who comes out poly increases the likelihood that others will become aware of their own poly identity and feel safe disclosing it. The more of us who take the risk of being openly and responsibly polyamorous, the sooner the confusion between uncommitted promiscuity or swinging, and committed multiple partner relationships will be clarified. The more of us who come out, the more easily we will be able to find and support each other.

When a critical mass of polyamorous people have come out, the outmoded paradigm of sexualove as a scarce and jealously guarded resource will shift. A new paradigm will emerge in which sexualove is an abundant and renewable gift of grace.

SHOULD I COME OUT?

We've been focusing here on the benefits of coming out, and indeed, one of the purposes of this book is to encourage more polys to come forward. I, myself, haven't experienced any problems resulting from my having been very outspoken on the subject of polyamory. In fact, I would have to say that it's enhanced and enriched my life in innumerable ways.

I've made many friends and encountered many fascinating people as a consequence of my organizing efforts in the polyamorous community. My older daughter found my very public polyamorous lovestyle embarrassing when she was a young teenager, but she went on to graduate from college with high honors and is now a delightful, responsible young adult. My younger daughter, who has never known anything other than polyamorous family life, enjoys the diversity of friends and lovers who share our lives. The rest of my family has been quite accepting of my chosen lovestyle.

It's been quite rare for a potential lover to be put off by my disclosure of polyamory, and I haven't lost any old friends—some find it hard to understand while others have been intrigued enough to follow my lead. I have to admit that I've sidestepped the career issue by choosing to stay outside of mainstream psychology, and I know that I'm having much more fun than I would in an academic or medical setting.

My own experience has been that my decision to come out was the best decision I ever made. The negative impact has been almost nonexistent, even after appearing on national television and radio programs. People in general have proven to be much more accepting than I ever expected. I also notice that when I'm with people with whom I haven't yet come out, I feel uncomfortable and guarded. But I have no doubt prevented many difficulties by choosing to live in a very tolerant and diverse part of the country, by choosing partners who share my beliefs and by choosing a lifestyle with a lot of flexibility.

Depending upon your situation, you may experience some losses and rejections if you come out to others. If you are married to an ardent monogamist, you are probably in for some intense processing as we discussed in Chapter 6. If your family has trouble accepting your autonomy, they may not be very enthusiastic about your news. If you are a minister, school teacher or politician you may need to exercise considerable discretion—or find a new career. If you live in a highly conservative part of the country, you may want to relocate.

The reality is that coming out *can* have a dramatic impact on your life, and only you can decide which risks are worth taking. But I strongly urge every self-identified poly reading this to at least *take the first step and come out to someone.* Taking this first step will help you decide what to do next.

In general, the sooner you begin your coming out process, the easier it will be for you to build a life that truly reflects who you are. The younger you are, the less likely you are to have created structures in your life which will have to be dismantled if you come out. But most of us go through developmental crises throughout our adult lives. Take advantage of your next milestone to begin creating the lovestyle you want.

HOW TO COME OUT

Your next step in coming out will depend on your individual circumstances and needs, but nearly everyone can benefit from reviewing their own history and asking themselves these questions:

When did you first have more than one lover or
    boy/girlfriend at a time?
When did you first recognize that you were poly?
How did you feel about it?
What did you decide about letting others know you were polyamorous?
When did you first meet another person who was poly?
Who was the first person you came out to? What exactly did you say?
How did they respond?
Who else have you told? Not told? Why?

Next review the important people in your life and ask:

How honest have I been with person x,y and z? (Don't forget to include yourself!)
How honest do I want to be with person x,y and z?
How risky does it feel to be more honest with person x,y and z?

If it feels too risky to let *anyone* know that you are poly, you probably still feel that you're doing something wrong. Find a support group or an open-minded therapist to explore some of these issues. Start a journal in which you can privately record your feelings and experiences. Try answering personal ads and talking to strangers who know nothing else about you, so that you can start fresh.

The following exercise is a good way to map out your own individual route to poly liberation.

Shine the light of television into your closet. Imagine that you've just received a phone call from the producers of a national talk show. They want to know if you'll appear as a guest to talk about your polyamorous lovestyle. "And could you bring any of your lovers with you?" they ask. You take a deep breath and tell them you'll have to think about it. They say they'll get back to you in a few days.

Now ask yourself, what is your greatest fear about appearing on this talk show? What questions might be asked that you wouldn't want to answer on national television? What would be hard to explain? What might you feel embarrassed or ashamed about? What would you be most proud of? Who would or would not be willing to accompany you? Who would you be afraid would see you? What would you not want them to find out about you? What consequences (negative or positive) might result from your appearance on the show?

Try to write down at least some of your answers. Now ask yourself, what would have to change in your life for you to feel comfortable appearing on this TV show? What would be the easiest to change? The hardest?

We realize that for some people, a complete answer to the questions above would be longer than this entire book. But it is a very effective way to see what work you need to do, as we've found out each time we've been asked to make a public appearance.

Now that you've identified some next steps for yourself, try the letter writing exercise below.

Write a coming out letter. Choose someone from your cast of characters to whom you would like to, but have not yet, come out. If possible, choose a pivotal person such as a lover, parent, or close friend. Then begin by telling this person about your positive feelings toward them. Tell them how much you value your relationship with them and offer appreciation for their contributions to your life. If you're writing to someone whom you have mixed feelings toward, or who you feel has wronged you or misunderstood you in the past, such as a parent or ex-spouse, be careful not to blame them or judge them for what they've done. Instead, tell them about the hurt that you've felt and how you've tried to protect yourself from feeling that hurt. Then share whatever you can about being polyamorous and proud. If you know that the person you're writing to is an ardent monogamist, be sure to emphasize that you respect their choices and you'd like them to respect yours.

If you feel ready to take the risk, mail the letter. If you don't, ask yourself: *What might I gain from sharing this letter? What might I lose?*

The letter on the next page was written by Susan Robins on National Coming Out Day 1991 and mailed to her young adult sons. Susan is a former school teacher and housewife who has been actively exploring polyamory for many years.

Dear Joey and Jeff,

Twenty years ago Daddy and I traveled through this same part of Rhode Island when I was pregnant with Jeff and Joey was only two. Our marriage was full of ups and downs as marriages are, because neither of us knew ourselves well enough back then to be truly honest about "who we are."

We followed the usual pattern of settle down, get married and have kids. We didn't have sexual intercourse before we got married, even though I was 21 years old. And we really didn't settle down. We moved from place to place, always with a sense of looking and longing for both of us. For myself, I know now I wanted more variety of sex in my life. I especially wanted to experience making love with a woman. I would fantasize that someone I had met in the supermarket or at church or school was in bed with us. I always wanted Dad to be there too. I would talk to him about it and I think sometimes he was turned on by my fantasies, even though he said he didn't approve.

With one couple we had an ongoing fantasy that we shared about building a house together with one kitchen and two master bedrooms, and lots of space for our six children. We spent hours and hours dreaming about the possibility of this with the Johnson's. I now realize that part of that dream for me was to fully actualize that relationship, and make love with both Joyce and Peter.

Now Daddy and I are going on separate paths. I have found people who support the ideas of group marriage and polyamory—people who have helped me to accept my nonmonogamous self. I know I am capable of loving more than one person, just as I love both of you boys and your sister too.

The decision to "come out" to you has not been an easy one. I have talked to your sister about all of this before. Somehow it was simpler to tell her than to tell you, but now that I have written this letter I feel much better, like a load has been lifted from my shoulders.

I will always love both of you and Dad and your sister and all of our large families. I feel I have a capacity for loving that has not yet found—and may never find—it's limits.

Love as always,

Mom

Chapter 8

CB

FINDING YOUR TRIBE

"Decide to network
Use every letter you write
Every conversation you have
Every meeting you attend
To express your fundamental beliefs and dreams
Affirm to others the vision of the world you want"
Robert Muller for The Networking Institute

If you are like most people who have found that multipartner relationships suit them better than monogamy, you often feel very isolated, alone and unappreciated. In a culture which assumes that monogamy–or more accurately, serial monogamy–is the only legitimate option for intimate relationships, many polyamorous people soon learn to stay safely in the closet. Unfortunately, as we discussed in the last chapter, closets are notoriously poor places to meet people.

Gays and lesbians, swingers, even bisexuals have managed to create viable subcultures. However, those of us who want committed, long-term relationships which are not limited to being in a couple often find ourselves at a loss when it comes to contacting others of like mind. Do not despair! While polyamorous people are a definite minority in our society, with a little effort and a lot of persistence, you too can find your tribe.

Since the first edition of this book was published in 1992 a great deal of progress has been made in establishing an international network of polyamorous people. In fact, you will find that there are now several polyamorous or poly-friendly global networks, as well as dozens of local groups, each with their own unique flavor. While the growing poly subculture may not be very visible yet outside of a few leading edge places, it's been a definite reality in my life for nearly a decade.

In fact, I've begun to be concerned that tendencies toward poly separatism, poly factions, and poly correctness may be unhealthy manifestations of the emerging polyamorous community. If you've never seen so much as a trickle of polyamorous culture, you may not be terribly worried about this kind of over zealous approach to poly identity. So by all means, enjoy your journey home. If you are one of the many polyamorous people who quietly live their lives without feeling the need or desire to make a big deal out of being polyamorous, more power to you. Whatever your personal proclivities, please remember that our goal is to overcome the stigma and sanctions that make it dangerous for people to be openly polyamorous and therefore difficult to find others of like mind. Hopefully we can do so without creating yet another niche for those who are invested in claiming victimized minority group status.

A SHORT HISTORY OF THE MODERN POLYAMORY MOVEMENT

Some people have always had multiple lovers and twentieth century individuals are no exception. Those who choose to ignore public opinion have done it quite openly: artists such as Picasso, Hollywood stars such as Madonna, or philosophers such as Carl Jung to name a few. Politicians, princes, and generals as well as ordinary citizens usually choose to keep their polyamorous personal affairs secret.

Throughout history various individuals have raised the battle cry for liberation from the tyranny of monogamy. Some of the more illustrious crusaders in this century include Nobel Laureate Bertrand Russell[1], political activist Emma Goldman, philosopher Dane Rudhyar[2], and spiritual teacher Bhagwan Shree Rajneesh[3]. All of these have had a profound impact in their own way, but in terms of the lineage of the modern day polyamory movement, at least in the United States of America, I think it's safe to say that it really began to take shape as a mass movement with the publication of two best selling books which influenced millions of people.

Robert Heinlein's *Stranger in a Strange Land* (1961) and Robert Rimmer's *Harrad Experiment* (1966) in addition to firing the imaginations of countless individuals, both led directly to the formation of grass roots support groups with a human potential flavor all across the country. Heinlein's *Stranger* was the inspiration for the neo-pagan Church of All World's founded by Oberon Zell which now has "nests" from coast to coast as well as abroad. Rimmer's *Harrad Experiment* (which was followed by many more novels and collections of letters and articles about polyamory) catalyzed countless experiments as well as the formation of numerous regional networks, some of which are still active today.

Meanwhile, the publication of Rusty and Della Roy's seminal non-fiction work, *Honest Sex* in 1967 set in motion a chain of events leading to the Kirkridge Sexuality Conferences which served to network polyamorous clergy, researchers, writers, and artists on the East coast[4]. The Kirkridge Conferences led to the establishment of a Los Angeles community called Sandstone by John and Barbara Williamson in the early '70's which in turn provided many human potential leaders and other adventurous souls with a taste of polyamorous community. Throughout the '70's

books, newsletters, even Hollywood movies, explored the
concept of nonmonogamous relationships.

When I came on the scene in the early 80's the advent of
AIDS and the Reagan era had led *Time Magazine* to declare
that the Sex Revolution was over and most people were
scurrying back to the safety of monogamy. Although a few
polyamorous support groups founded in the '70's such as
Family Synergy in Los Angeles and Family Tree in Boston
still existed, their memberships were both aging and
shrinking and all but invisible to the general public. The
infamous Kerista commune continued to dominate the San
Francisco nonmonogamy scene with their prolific utopian
writings, but few people could swallow the whole Kerista
trip and there wasn't much room for disagreement.

I decided to start IntiNet (having no idea that Internet would
soon become a major buzz word) as a national organization
for polyamorous people, as well as a local support group,
following my first television appearance on *Donahue* in 1984.
Our networking was still so low profile that I didn't learn
that Ryam Nearing had founded Polyfidelitous Educational
Productions (PEP) around the same time until we met on
the set of the Playboy Channel's *Women on Sex* talk show a
year later. The movement grew at a snail's pace throughout
the '80's and by 1988 I was sufficiently burned out to turn
my energies to building my own family.

The advent of accessible desktop publishing in the early '80's
led to the publication of *Love Without Limits* and the revival
of the IntiNet newsletter, *Floodtide*, in 1992. PEP had made
similar strides during this time, and the growth of these two
organizations along with the expansion of the Internet gave
rise to the re-emergence of today's Polyamory Movement.
After many years of intensive effort, the disparate pieces of

the network began to come together. The older and younger poly activists began to collaborate, the East and West coast contingents connected, and Ryam Nearing and I joined forces to create *Loving More Magazine* which replaced our separate newsletters and provided the movement with a national magazine.

All this activity has established a solid base for you to start finding your tribe. One possibility is for you to begin as I did, by starting your own support group. If a support group for polyamorists seems too threatening for your circumstances, or too limiting for your broader interests, you could consider organizing a salon or discussion group focused on more general issues pertaining to alternatives for families, conscious relationships or intentional community. Once you establish some trust with this group, you could come out to them and find out if there are others of like mind who are also hiding out.

If this sounds like too much work, you might prefer to meet others by attending one of our *Love Without Limits* workshops or one of the regional polyamory conferences. Or you may prefer to start by participating in an on-line discussion group or polyamory newsgroup on the Internet. If you don't have access to a computer and a modem, you can always start with polyamorous pen pals. In any case, whoever you are and whatever your situation, you can reach out and link up with others who believe as you do.

WORKSHOPS AND CONFERENCES

Attending an event for polyamorous people is probably the quickest and easiest way to create an experience for yourself of living in a polyamorous culture. The *Love Without Limits* workshops provide a structured process for up to thirty-six people to take a journey into group intimacy for an evening, a day, a weekend, or sometimes longer. Each of our workshops has a different focus, but they all balance the functions of body, mind, emotions, and sexuality using some of the eight steps to polyamory outlined earlier. Information on how to contact us to receive our current schedule can be found at the back of this book.

These events are appropriate for people who are partnered or single, but if you have one or more partners, we strongly recommend that you attend together in order to get the maximum benefit. Sometimes people in committed couples are afraid that jealousy will arise if they attend together, or they want the opportunity to explore new relationships alone, but part of our purpose here is to bring these issues to the surface in a safe environment where you will be supported in working through them.

You may also wish to attend a larger gathering, conference, or camp where you can have a sense of belonging to a tribe of hundreds of polyamorous people. These large conferences usually offer less intimacy and support than a small workshop, but they do enable you to meet many more people and experience the tremendous diversity of the polyamorous community. I will never forget the excitement of the first really large polyamory conference (really large in polyamory land means over one hundred people) which was held on the University of California at Berkeley campus in the early '90's. We drove up to the entrance to find people lined up all the way down the block waiting to get in. I'd never seen so many polyamorous people in one place before! The Internet is probably the best way to find out when and where these events are being held.

MEETING OTHERS ONLINE

Even before the advent of the World Wide Web, online conferences, newsgroups, and mailing lists began creating virtual community for widely scattered polyamorous people all around the world. In my opinion, electronic community can not come close to the real flesh and blood, eye to eye experience, but if you live in some out of the way place, you no longer need feel isolated and alone if you have access to a computer and a modem.

Now, all you have to do is enter the word "polyamory" in your search engine to instantly connect with dozens of online polyamory resources on the Web. These range from individual web pages to personals ads to social or intellectual dialogues. By the time you read this you may be able to access our website at *http:\\www.lovewithoutlimits.com*. The *Loving More Magazine* website can be found at *http:\\www.lovemore.com* and is another major gateway to polyamory on the Web. Just be sure to familiarize yourself with the rules of the road before venturing out into cyberspace or you may get flamed.

STARTING A SUPPORT GROUP

None of the previous options compares to your own local support group in terms of the potential for both ongoing rewards and ongoing hard work. Before you begin to form your support group, you will need to make a few basic decisions. The clearer your intentions, the better your chances are of ending up with a group which meets your needs. First, you need to decide on the scope and focus of your group. Will you accept members who are pursuing any alternative to monogamy (i.e., open relationships, intimate networks, patriarchal polygamy, swinging, polyfidelity, group marriage, etc.), or will you limit the group to people who have chosen a particular option? Also, will your members include those who are merely curious, those with a serious or long-term interest or only those with some real life experience?

Next, you must determine the primary purpose of your group. Do you want a safe place to discuss problems and concerns in inclusive relationships, a place to explore and formulate your notions of ideal relationships or a platform for building your own expanded family? Do you want a loose network which includes as many people as possible with no strings attached, or do you want a committed group whose goal is to become increasingly intimate and to help its members acquire new interpersonal skills?

Will you sponsor any sexually permissive events at which group members may interact sexually or will you stick to talking, dancing, and friendly hugs? Are you willing to serve as a dating club for singles and couples seeking either long-term mates or short-term playmates? If a dating club is not your goal, you will have to screen potential members carefully, because you will certainly attract cruisers. These possibilities are not mutually exclusive, but different priorities will result in different types of groups.

Take a few minutes now to complete the following statements:

1. *The primary purpose of this support group is to . . .*
2. *This support group will be open to members who . . .*
3. *The work of organizing and running this support group will be handled by . . .*
4. *The cost of participating in this support group will be . . .*
5. *The feeling tone of this support group will be . . .*

Now you are ready to tackle the logistics:

Where will you meet?
How often?
At what time?
What kind of format will you have?
Will you have an ongoing or a drop-in group?

We have found that a monthly potluck dinner followed by a meditation or drumming circle and group discussion works well, but you will have to decide what's best for you. Once you have answered the questions above, you are ready to begin looking for members.

FINDING OTHERS

Word-of-mouth. As you may already be aware, the best way to get the word out about anything, anywhere, is through word-of-mouth. However, as a lone polyamorist you are probably convinced that this approach will get you nowhere. Either you have already found through bitter experience that none of your friends wants to hear about your aberrant sexual desires, or you are afraid of alienating the people close to you by opening the subject. It may well take some time before word-of-mouth will serve you. Nevertheless, we urge you to consider taking a risk and talking with any prospects you may have in your personal network. Even if your direct contacts are less than enthusiastic, they may know of someone else who is very interested. In any case you will get some practice in describing your proposed support group. Of course, you will have to use your judgement about whom to approach, but you may be pleasantly surprised.

A success story. Paul was cautious, at first, about mentioning his interest in polyamory to his co-workers. But eventually he did bring it up with a fellow he was working very closely with. Bill's response was pretty unremarkable— he was neither shocked nor intrigued. But over a year later, Paul received an urgent phone call from another colleague, Bob, whom he knew only slightly. Bob, it turned out, had been sailing with Bill and had been bemoaning the difficulties he'd been having finding other polyamorous people. Bill recalled his conversation with Paul and suggested that Bob give him a call. Paul was delighted to find that there was another polyamorist at his company and arranged a evening phone appointment to talk further. Paul was even more delighted when, on phoning Bob's home that evening, he learned that Patricia, another co-worker whom he'd found very attractive, was Bob's partner. Bob and Patricia were thrilled to hear there was a local support group and a national conference coming up soon.

Existing Organizations. Your next best bet is to check out the membership of national or regional groups devoted to alternatives to monogamy. See the *Organizational Directory* at the end of this book or check out the Internet for suggestions on which ones to contact. Some of these groups publish listings of members trying to find partners and some sponsor annual gatherings. Several have informative publications which may contain information about existing local support groups. You should also network with any other groups in your community who may have a high percentage of interested members. Some possibilities include organizations for alternative healers, massage therapists, bisexuals, pagans, Unitarians, New Age churches, sanyasins, permaculture, contact improvisational dance, rebirthers, libertarians, civil liberties advocates, Mensans, tantrikas and other alternative movements.

Advertising. Strategically placed classified ads are likely to produce the greatest volume of response, but many of the respondents will probably be inappropriate for your group. If you are willing to spend time screening applicants, and you have—or are willing to develop—the skills, this method can work well. Run your ad for at least four weeks before evaluating the results. The longer it runs, the better your response will be. Below is the copy for two ads run by a local support group. Feel free to borrow from it.

BEYOND SINGLES, BEYOND COUPLES . . . Do you want more? Group marriage/expanded family may be what you're looking for. Support group for domestic pioneers open to new members. For further information send S.A.S.E. to....

RELATIONSHIPS FOR THE 90s . . . Expanded Family Network is a discussion/support group (monthly potluck) for those interested in creating/nourishing committed, multipartner, loving relationships—the safer, healthier alternative to the crumbling nuclear family. Free information packet from ....

SCREENING

We recommend that you request responses be sent to a post office box. You may want to ask respondents to reply with an essay about the reason for their interest in your group or you may want them to complete a questionnaire you develop for screening purposes. Alternatively, you may want to send them a longer description of your proposed group before taking the next step. Whatever you do, respond promptly to all inquiries or you will risk losing credibility.

These precautions will help sift through the inevitable

mismatches. You can be sure that swingers will respond to your ad even if you make it clear that you are not sponsoring a swing group. Also, be forewarned that the image of a warm, loving, multiadult family is naturally appealing to anyone who has not been socialized to reject it. You will most likely trigger responses from people whose mental and social functioning is deficient in ways that limit their ability to participate in a support group. We also prefer to screen out people with uncontrolled substance abuse problems. Do yourself a favor and limit your group to people who have one primary problem—being polyamorous in a monogamous culture. Follow-up the written contact with a lengthy phone conversation before initiating a face-to-face meeting.

Screening prospective members can be time consuming, but it's well worth the effort especially when your group is first forming. One difficult person can easily scare away a dozen more congenial types particularly if you have an inexperienced facilitator who doesn't have the skills to firmly but gently confront—and if necessary eject—a troublesome group member.

On the other hand, you don't want to screen too rigorously. One support group screening committee became so zealous that they rejected a triad who had been together for over five years because they questioned the triad's commitment to forming expanded family.

How can you tell who will make a good support group member? First, trust your intuition. Secondly, look for people who are able to talk about themselves, who can carry on a conversation with some give-and-take, who are assertive but not aggressive, and who are not afraid to express some emotion. Previous experience–in some other kind of group, in peer counseling or psychotherapy, or in a large and supportive extended family–is very helpful. Finally, consider a candidate's relationship history. Someone who has never had a committed intimate relationship (unless they are very young) is unlikely to make a good group member.

Now, where to place your ad? Most metropolitan areas have alternative weekly newspapers with popular "personals" sections. Many cities also have one or more publications for singles. You may need to convince an editor that you are offering a legitimate service, but give it a try. If you live in a rural or very conservative area, you will obviously have more difficulty, but perhaps you can find a regional publication which will accept your ad. Or you can always consider moving to another part of the country!

Another possibility is to place a classified ad in a national alternative magazine with a large circulation. This will be a little more costly, but perhaps you can network with contact people from several different areas to sponsor some co-operative ads. Of course, you will want to place a listing in *Loving More Magazine*, but it's unlikely that this alone will generate enough responses to form a group.

If you live in a progressive area, you may get good results from flyers posted in places like health food stores, Unitarian (or other liberal) churches, holistic health centers, sexual information centers, alternative bookstores, libraries or college campuses. One support group has used a very clever flyer which lists the titles of some classic science fiction books dealing with multiple partner relationships. The titles wouldn't mean much to the average person, but are immediately recognizable to anyone with a serious interest in polyamory.

Finally, be sure to provide any relevant community switch-boards or referral networks with information sheets. Marriage and family counselors and psychotherapists may also be willing to tell interested clients about your group.

If you are really adventurous, you can approach some radio talk show hosts about putting you on the air. Broadcast media can generate a huge response, but we haven't had much luck with finding quality people in this way.

MEETING FORMATS

We have found that it works well to divide our meetings into business and support portions. It's also a good idea to try some activity-oriented meetings—i.e., hiking, picnicking, swimming or dancing. You will want to involve everyone, if possible, in planning future meetings and recruiting new members. If your concept is to create a grass roots, low or no cost group run by volunteers, make it clear from the beginning that this is a group effort and requires that everyone take responsibility for making it happen. Otherwise, you will eventually burn out on doing all the work yourself and the group will not be sustainable.

We usually begin with a quiet or meditation time to gather and focus the group energy, followed by introductions or a brief "check-in" if there are no new people present. Starting a meeting with singing, drumming, and/or dancing can also be a very effective way to build community. It works well to have several discussion topics to suggest to the group, or you can use an interactive exercise or bring in a guest speaker. You can also ask us to loan you a video of a talk show featuring polyamorous guests being thrown to the lions.

After you've been meeting for a while, you may want to

allow time to handle any conflicts which come up between group members. Any group which continues over a period of time needs to develop a conflict resolution process. Otherwise disgruntled members are likely to pick up their marbles and go home. Since your goal is to bring people together, you will want to reach agreement about how conflicts will be resolved before they come up. Or contact us to create a special workshop to help your group breakthrough to a higher level of synergy.

Before you begin, it's best to agree on some ground rules for the group. At minimum, these should include:

1) *confidentiality*–nothing discussed in the group is to be repeated outside the group in a way which might possibly identify the people involved without their explicit permission.
2) *respect*–everyone has a right to speak and be listened to without criticism or judgement; use "I statements" to express disagreement, i.e., "I don't see it that way," not "You're wrong."
3) *punctuality*–begin and end on time.
4) *attendance*–if your group is an ongoing one with an agenda of increasing intimacy and personal growth, you may want to have an agreement about regular attendance.

We strongly recommend that you have a group facilitator for each meeting, and that you rotate this duty among all group members. You can pair a more experienced with a less experienced person if necessary. You may want to follow the group portion with some unstructured time, but it's nice to bring the group back together for closing comments or a group hug.

For business meetings it's also a good idea to take notes of important decisions and action plans and circulate them so every one remembers what has been agreed upon. Some groups make all decisions by consensus, that is, everyone must be in full agreement on the decision. This tends to be more time consuming than a simple majority vote or hierarchical system, but it also leads to better group dynamics in the long run.

Be careful not to let old habits of domination and competition or helplessness and care taking creep into your business meetings. Maintain an atmosphere of harmony and cooperation. Keep it simple and keep it fun. Remember, this group is here to support each other, so find a way to do it that works for everyone!

THE "LOOK MA, NO HANDS" APPROACH

If all this discussion about recruiting, organizing meetings, screening, and rules sounds like too much work and not enough fun, you may want to try a more informal approach to finding your tribe. If you are fortunate enough to live in an area where it's easy to meet lots of people (perhaps because others have already laid the groundwork by establishing lively gathering places and events) and you know how to engage with them in a meaningful way, you may be able to create a polyamorous network around you with less effort.

Simply use your intuition to identify people who are on your wavelength, get to know each other, meet each other's friends, and start spending time together. If you are all open to being real with each other and being honest about your needs and if you share an intention to work through any fears which arise, you can form a tribe more spontaneously.

Chapter 9

❧

BUILDING YOUR FAMILY

> *"The complexity of a system is limited only if the system is rigid, inflexible and isolated from its environment. Self-organizing systems in continual interaction with their environment are capable of tremendously increasing their complexity by abandoning structural stability in favor of flexibility and open-ended evolution."*
> Erich Jantsch, *Design for Evolution*

Some people find themselves in a multimate family or intimate network without having consciously chosen to create one. But because such arrangements are far outside our cultural norms, many more people first become dissatisfied with the status quo and then get the idea they'd like to have several partners. At this point, they usually realize that they haven't any idea how to proceed. It's also common for people to have a taste of the polyamorous experience which turns out to be quite short-lived. But having experienced it, however briefly, they begin to realize that there can be more to love than just being in an exclusive couple and they are unwilling to settle for less. Finally, there are also triads and larger groups of committed partners who would like to increase their family size still further. All of these groups may find that creating an intentional family is easier said than done.

How can you find, attract and select compatible partners for a multimate family or an intimate network? Unfortunately, there aren't any simple answers to that question. I have been learning by trial and error for a couple of decades so by this time I have experimented with just about every possible way of forming family. I've also examined the histories of other domestic pioneers. Over the years I've realized that getting attached to a particular idea of how it's supposed to be can actually be an obstacle to allowing your family to grow organically. It's generally been quite easy for me to create an abundance of friends and lovers in my life. What has been much more challenging is to gather an aligned, compatible group of people who are as attracted to each other as they are to me. Nevertheless, I find that if I really tune in to myself and express who I am to those around me, the family creation process naturally becomes activated and takes on a life of its own which may or may not conform to my expectations.

My observation is that multiple partner lovestyles have much potential both for enhancing the dance of life and for wreaking havoc. Perhaps the complexity of orchestrating these lovestyles is nature's way of guarding against the misuse of power by people who are ill-equipped to handle the tremendous energies unleashed by synergistic love. For unlike simple dyadic relationships which operate as units of two whether they are exclusive or inclusive, in a new paradigm expanded family group each member must independently, of their own free will, choose each other, surrender their egos, and make it a priority to bond with each other. This is why guru-led, old paradigm families in which everyone's primary bond is with the group leader are so much more common than egalitarian ones. And herein lies one of those puzzling paradoxes. New paradigm intentional families rarely come into being by accident, but at the same time, one person or couple can not make it happen by sheer force of will.

There is no single right way to build a multipartner family, just as there is no single right form that such a relationship must take. We are using the term *family* to refer to any committed group of sexualoving partners who feel that they are a family whether or not they all live together or consider themselves married to each other.   Historically, the polyamory movement has given more credence to "traditional" families, particularly those who are polyfidelitous, that is, those who fit the cultural patterns for the nuclear family except that they have more than two primary partners. As you will see from some of the stories below, our refusal to honor the experience of being bonded to others because the form of the relationship doesn't fit our picture of how a family should look can deprive us of the joy of knowing that we do belong to a living family.

At the same time, it's important to be aware that while some people limit the use of the word family to those who are married or related by blood and are living together, others use it very loosely, more as a synonym for network or special interest community or tribe. In general, I think we run the risk of reflecting in ourselves the image of the very same mono-cultural police whose tyranny we seek to escape, when we begin to set out correct definitions for family. However, it's also the case that communication can be quite confusing when the same word means different things to different people.

For purposes of this discussion, I will use the word *family* to mean a group of committed friends and lovers and their children, whether they take the form of an intimate network or a group marriage. In contrast, I think of tribes as being larger than families, perhaps including several interlocking families and/or a few dozen loosely related individuals. In my mind, networks and communities encompass many different levels of relationship and their members are less clearly identifiable than a family. They may include people who know each other only slightly but who share a common interest or value system, as well as those who are more intimately related. In any case, much of the following discussion of expanded families applies equally well to tribes, networks, and intentional communities.

I hope that by outlining some of the issues involved, I can help you navigate this mysterious territory. Over the years I've found that some approaches consistently fail while others are more promising. You may be the exception that proves the rule, but I offer my observations about what usually works and what doesn't in hopes of saving you the tiresome and troubling necessity of reinventing the wheel.

STARTING FROM SQUARE ONE

The issues that single people face in building a family are often quite different from those faced by couples or triads. In some ways the process is much simpler for singles who don't have to balance the demands of an existing primary relationship with the intricacies of new and unfamiliar configurations. On the other hand, singles may feel too needy and vulnerable as the "odd person out" relating to a couple to find the courage to proceed. Perhaps this is why many single people are convinced that in order to create an expanded family they must first become part of a couple.

While it's generally easier to become intimate with one partner than with several, if you are currently single, think twice before single-mindedly setting off in pursuit of a primary partner. Of course, if you should serendipitously stumble across the perfect mate for you, don't let a fantasy of plural possibilities hold you back. Just be aware that further expansion may not be on the immediate horizon. I've come to believe that a focus on building expanded family is generally not appropriate for a "new" couple. And by "new," I mean a couple who has been together for less than ten years.

What I've seen in my own dyadic relationships and those of others—and in more than one triadic relationship as well, is that the process of becoming a unit takes time and has a trajectory of its own. Until a couple or triad reaches the stage where the partners have worked out most of their internal issues and are ready to go beyond their existing identity as a couple, they may share many sexual adventures and even meaningful friendships with others, but they are not really fully available to create family with others. In the past, this process seems to have required a minimum of ten years, often much longer.

Even when a couple is developmentally ready to expand, even when they already have an open marriage, it's still a major transition to get to the next level of sensing themselves as bonded but separate individuals who are not subtly owned by each other or responsible for each other's feelings. Rare individuals may find themselves immune to the cultural programming which tells us that members of a couple have special privileges and obligations which are not shared by others, but most couples have a tremendous amount of conditioning to overcome before they are really able to expand their boundaries.

Couples often hope to find another compatible couple in order to form a happy foursome without upsetting their dyadic symmetry. While this may sound like an appealing idea in theory, in practice these arrangements are often relatively short-lived. What often happens is that one member of the couple will bond more strongly with their new partner(s) than the other, upsetting the dyadic balance which was a motivating factor in the first place. At this point, the couples may separate back into the original twosomes in an effort to regain some stability, or one couple may split up and a triad will be formed. Unlike the four person group or fourple, triads formed in this way often last for many years.

For those of you who are already involved in healthy, satisfying couples or triads, by all means stick it out and work through the issues you need to face in order to bond with others. If you are in a conflict-filled, dysfunctional relationship know that you will need to either heal or leave this relationship before you can make much progress in building your family. Don't deceive yourselves. If you're having trouble attracting others it may well be that the dynamic between you is repellent. No one will want to get caught in your cross fire.

It's fruitless to argue whether it's more difficult to work through the fears and barriers which keep couples isolated in nuclear families or whether it's more difficult for singles to overcome the powerful programming to find their own personal soulmate instead of accepting a hand-me-down and shared partner. In any case, polyamorous singles and couples both have to face the same kinds of fears regarding intimacy and commitment that monogamous people do and often with even greater intensity.

The bottom line is that where ever you're starting from is just right for you. Your road may be longer or shorter depending upon how willing you are to confront your issues and move through them, but you can be sure that the process of forming a family will at times place you squarely between a rock and a hard place. Whatever your circumstances, you must navigate carefully. Only scrupulous honesty with yourself and others can safely guide you. If you are seeking an opportunity to learn to let go of your ego-driven agendas and trust, you will be richly rewarded whatever the outcome. If you're determined to follow a pre-ordained plan, frustration most likely awaits you.

Let's turn now to the story of how three people who've been "married" to each other for more than two decades first got together. Several additional partners have joined them over the years, but they say their relationship really hasn't changed much since they first broke through their monogamous conditioning.

THE BIRTH OF A GROUP MARRIAGE

David and Kathy had been together for nearly ten years when they decided something important was missing from their lives. They were successful in their careers and felt that they had a reasonably good relationship. "Reasonably rotten as we see it now," David laughs. "But back then we thought, we haven't cut each other's throats yet, we must be doing okay."

Vowing to somehow find an alternative to lives of quiet desperation, David and Kathy sold everything they owned, quit their jobs and set off on a spiritual search. "We knew that there was something more to life, but we didn't know what it would look like," Kathy mused. "Six months later we ended up in Belize, where we met Sarah and Mike who were in pretty much the same place. The four of us came together with the purpose of putting our heads together, and we set aside a period of time for working very intensively on ourselves. The context for that was total openness, no secrets and no withholds on any level. We were all each other's grist for the mill. Part of that was sexuality. It became very clear to us that sexuality was appropriate between us, and that it was an area where we needed clearing. We discovered there's so much energy tied up in sex and it's not available if we're not clear."

"David and I had had other sexual partners earlier in our relationship. I guess you could say we had an open marriage. But group marriage just wasn't part of our experience up to that point. We had read Stranger in a Strange Land and resonated with it, but it wasn't just that we were trying this experiment where you swap wives. It was the context of working on ourselves that gave us the impetus to go through with handling the jealousy or possessiveness or whatever reactiveness we came up against."

"We had reached Belize," David added, "in a place of realizing that, look, nothing so far has worked. There must be more to life that this. We were willing to pull out all the stops, throw out all the morays, all the belief systems, because that's the only thing that's going to work. This is a last ditch effort. And in that spirit there are no givens, no should list. Whatever we see coming up we need to deal with, we need to cleanse. For that reason we isolated ourselves totally from society in a remote, isolated village. We were truly out of space and time and were able slowly but surely to let go of all our belief systems and programming. We needed to start from scratch."

"I had been a classic overachiever," Sarah chimed in. "Mike and I thought we were hot stuff, we were going to run a TV network or something like that. We were beginning to be successful in our careers and took a look ahead and saw what successful people looked like and it didn't look good. They were really unhappy, miserable human beings. So we said, ' This isn't it. I don't know what is, but lets go find out.' Up until then we'd led very conventional lives. An inheritance allowed us to drop out of the work force. We traveled for awhile and had lots of adventures. Then we met David and Kathy.

My sexual relationship with Mike was deteriorating and neither one of us knew what to do about it. We had gotten married under parental pressure and had already started contemplating affairs but weren't being honest about it. So opening up to sexuality with David and Kathy was part of the mind blower. But the first part was the synergy of us being together. The moment we met I had an experience of my own power like I'd never had before in my life. At twenty-four, it was my first touch of what's real. And then to contemplate that sexual energy was part of that and could be shared cut through so much of my programming— everything I had to confront around unconditional love and open, inclusive sexuality."

"We didn't set out to reconceptualize sex and the role of sex in the entire human dilemma," David insists. "But it kept coming up. We'd be exploring the nature of emotions and all of the sudden we'd find ourselves back at sex. We'd be having a lofty philosophical discussion of what truly is unconditional love and bam! straight up against sex. We'd be exploring some abstract concept and we'd come up against sex. It was literally looming its head at every turn. Until finally we realized that, oh, I get it, we have to handle this. Maybe this is bigger than we thought.

"What's happened in the last 4,000 years has been that we have unduly devalued the potency of sex as a positive spiritual energy. And what it came down to for us is that sex is spirit. Are we not talking about a fundamental life energy that connects us all? Is not the moment of orgasm the moment of enlightenment–an outrageous idea to us at the time. It was that kind of fresh, almost reluctant, discovery that kept coming up for us. So finally we said, all right, we have to go into it and out of that we really got solidified as a group marriage.

"We were looking for God and we kept finding sex. We thought, 'what are we, sex fiends? Oh my God, I'm going celibate and I choose to be celibate for the rest of my life.' But that's not the way to handle it either. It was our commitment to Truth that kept us going.

"We really haven't learned much about relationships since," David concluded. "Everything we are now was in place after a year and a half in Belize."

Sarah added, "What happened with the jealousy aspect was really important. Without that I wouldn't have been able to stay with Kathy and David when Mike left. After we left Belize, Mike wanted to go back to globe trotting. I wanted to continue in the direction the four of us had been headed. I loved Kathy and wanted the best for her. That seemed to be contradicting my basic programming of wanting it all for me. Discovering that when Kathy was making love with Mike there could be the possibility of my being jealous, but there was also this other experience I was having of isn't that wonderful, I love those two so much, it's so beautiful. But then thinking, I should be jealous. And out of that I realized that jealousy is not a given, it's not always going to be there. It's a choice, it's just one moment in time. And I could either leave it behind or carry it with me for a life time. It had never occurred to me that that was even a possibility. It gave me an enormous sense of freedom.

"And there was this real agreement that we were doing this thing together. So nobody was left in their jealousy. Almost every night we had a group communication where we were totally honest. We shared the things we don't usually share. So knowing I could share it with this loving attention and heal it instantly really helped.   Also we had real clear agreements that sex would be between all of us.   So ultimately it became clear that it doesn't matter if I'm there physically or not–I'm there. I'm always there.

"The issues around sexuality ran completely through my being. If I cleared something around sexual jealousy that cleared all possessiveness in the material realm."

"I was probably the lowest of the four in Jealousy Quotient," David admits, "but I still had to confront it. A few things really worked for me. First seeing that it was a choice, a cultural program.   There's no jealousy gene. Second, it didn't get the job done! It didn't bring Kathy closer to me, it alienated Kathy.   It didn't bring greater harmony, it distanced.   Third, the final step, I could experience the joy without being the direct participant. When the four of us were making love in one giant bed and Kathy was moaning with ecstasy, I would have waves of ecstasy come over me and yet I was with Sarah and we'd be in a different phase of our lovemaking but rather than having it be a distraction, I'd feel this wave come over me and go back out to Sarah. So I realized, I'm getting more, not less."

Hopefully we can profit from the hard-won wisdom of people like Kathy, David and Sarah as we wend our way across the trails they've blazed. Now let's take a look at the process of forming an intimate network.

MY OWN STORY

For over two decades I have been working in the laboratory of my own life to discover how I can love and be loved more fully, more freely, and more consciously. Having always been a highly erotic person, I've struggled for many years to fully integrate my sexuality with my emotional, spiritual, and intellectual life. Part of my path has been to discover how to open deeply to others without the props of exclusivity and ownership. Part of my path has been to discover how to catalyze group energies into viable communities of intimate equals, groups that do not rely on the presence of a guru for inspiration or leadership. It's been a long journey, full of surprises and flavored by both ecstasy and pain.

Sometimes it seems that I'm finally coming home. Sometimes it seems that I've gotten no where. But through it all I find that my most important ally is my faith in the truth of my own experience. The more I can allow myself to know that truth—regardless of its political correctness —and express it, the more I find myself on solid ground. Some of my ideas about love and relationship have changed since the first edition of this book was published, and I want you to know that they are still changing. At the same time, my deepest values, my dearest dreams, and my most magnetic attractions seem to stay the same over time. But as I grow in understanding, the expression of my core self does take different forms.

As I look back, I realize I have been building an intimate network over the last twenty-some years. This process started in 1975 about a year after I separated from my first husband and fell head over heels in love with Jack. When he first made love to me, I sensed he was worshipping the Divine. I literally saw stars. This was my first tantric initiation, and it changed my life forever. Alas, it quickly became apparent that Jack and I were not going to get married and live happily ever after. For one thing, I was about to leave the state to go to graduate school, and for another he'd informed me that he was nonmonogamous and had several girlfriends. Besides, we pushed each other's buttons so intensely, we really couldn't spend much time together. I was still very young and understood little about relating. At the same time, I knew that Jack had touched my soul so deeply I wanted him to stay in my life forever.

I realized I had a choice. I could transcend my jealousy and expectations and love him unconditionally or I could try to shut him out of my heart and forget about him. I chose to keep loving him, not knowing at the time where this would lead me. Several years later I married for the second time, trying to fit myself into the traditional mold with an ambitious, personable husband and a house with a white picket fence. He too had unfinished business with an old lover, but while continued friendships were acceptable to him, extra-marital love affairs were not. I was researching domestic violence for my doctoral dissertation at the time and was horrified to realize that the dynamics of domination, control, jealousy and dependency that I'd observed in the abusive marriages I was studying, existed, at a more moderate level, in my own marriage. Determined to find a way to love in alignment with my beliefs and life purpose, but still not knowing how it would look, I divorced again.

I soon became part of a group of renegade psychotherapists who met every two weeks for a couple of years. We would take turns leading the group, facilitating others, working on our own stuff, exploring the group mind, and creating innovative tools and combinations of tools to take us into new psychospiritual territory. We also fantasized about developing a more cooperative, communal lifestyle but this aspect never went as far as I hoped it would. Although many of us were in open relationships and some of us had partners within the group and exchanged or shared partners over time, we did not think of ourselves as polyamorous. In fact, my participation in this group predated my "coming out poly" by several years.

Nonetheless, Aaron, my primary lover at the time, and I were fascinated by the dynamics of triangular relationships of all kinds. We made it a point to experiment with them whenever possible, both in the group I just described and in other situations. Aaron introduced me to Damian, an acquaintance of his who was well versed in both pagan and tantric practices. I asked Damian to teach me tantra and he readily agreed. For the first time I began to see that the play of energy that spontaneously arose between me and some of my lovers could be deliberately invoked and channeled. Damian shared our passion for triangles, and soon Aaron, Damian, and I found ourselves exploring three-way sexual interactions. We also found ourselves tripped up, time and again by our gender roles. None of us had firm enough boundaries, none of us had done enough sexual healing, and even though we were relatively free of jealousy, none of us were free enough from our other conditioning to really connect with each other.

Toward the end of this period I met another man who, along with Jack, would eventually become part of my present intimate network. But it would still be many years before the seeds I planted way back then would bear fruit. Now, after many seasons of patiently—or often impatiently—waiting for individual relationships to deepen and for different parts of my network to come together it truly feels like a miracle every time old and new friends and lovers finally meet and connect with each other with a shared understanding of the possibility we have to weave our lives together. Of course, not everyone loves each other at first sight—though some do—but all are curious and excited about the journey we are taking.

Meanwhile, discouraged both by my inability to succeed at traditional marriage and my inability to do much more than apply psychological bandaids to the battered women and children who were casualties of our family institutions, I began to research alternatives to monogamy and the nuclear family. As luck would have it, practically the first people I encountered were the group whose beginnings are described in the previous section. By this time they had been together for over ten years and had grown to a core group of four with two more in the process of joining them full time. I learned a great deal by becoming part of this extended family, including all the basic principles of new paradigm relating. They reached out to me with such love and support, it would have been easy to let my quest end here, but I seemed to have a need to blaze my own trail so I continued building my network from scratch.

Richard was one of many intimate friends I made in the next few years and was also an important teacher for me. He came into my life at a time when I was relating to several different men who each brought out different parts of me. You might say I had a lover for each chakra. For the first time in my life, I was fully engaged on every level and as a result I attracted a man who could meet me on every level.

Richard had been in an open marriage for about twenty years and soon told me he was looking for a Number 2 wife. Our sexual, emotional and intellectual chemistry was extraordinary, and he was very skilled at making me feel special while clearly giving priority to his wife and children. We were all professional psychotherapists so were very conscious of the subtleties of our group dynamics. My position was similar to that of "the other woman" except that he didn't keep me secret from his wife. The three of us would sometimes hang out at their home or go out together, but she didn't seem open to developing much of a relationship with me. She told me once she'd seen too many of my counterparts come and go over the years to think I'd be around for long. Indeed, this was a passionate but stormy relationship which taught me a tremendous amount about open relating, but which ultimately proved to be an obstacle to creating an intimate network for myself.

Both Richard and David fit the profile for dominant or *alpha* males. They were mature, powerful men who knew their strengths and found it natural to take a leadership role. I enjoyed relating to this kind of man, but found that my other lovers felt competitive and overshadowed by them. While I felt blessed by the presence of sister-wives and wanted to further explore my bisexual nature, I knew that a situation where one man was being shared by a group of women wasn't going to mesh well with my sexual appetites.

At this point I'd been single for about seven years and while I enjoyed my intimate network, I was feeling the urge to bond more deeply and create a primary, live-in relationship for myself. I pictured a loving, gender-balanced family of four to six adults and several children (my daughter from my first marriage was now a teenager). I decided to begin by pairing up with a man who also wanted a group marriage and who expressed a strong desire for cooperative living. Perhaps the two of us could form the core for a larger group. For six years we thrived in our open marriage, but never succeeded in growing beyond the dyad. This marriage lasted longer and was generally an improvement on my monogamous marriages. Unfortunately my partner and I were frequently attracted to and found attractive by very different people. So even though we were aligned on many important life goals, building family together began to seem unrealistic.

Eventually I realized that whatever we might say or think to the contrary, the institution of marriage had had its way with us. I simply could not stay conscious enough to avoid being sucked in to the old Dominator stereotypes, even if monogamy was not an issue. Finally, I came to realize that polyamory is not enough to serve as a basis for marriage.

When I ended this marriage a few years ago, I was determined that I would not repeat my pattern of seeking refuge in a couple relationship of any description because I'd failed to create a viable expanded family. Luckily, I discovered that many former lovers who had drifted out of my life during my open marriage were still there for me in significant ways and ready to renew our connections. But once again, I found myself challenged to maintain my intimate network in the face of jealousy from first one, then another new lover.

These were men who'd initially been attracted to me because I was polyamorous, but who then "fell in love" and wanted the safety of an exclusive relationship, at least temporarily while their newly-in-love brain chemistry was engaged. If you want a monogamous commitment, find somebody else, I told them, knowing full well that they themselves had had plenty of negative experiences with serial monogamy. I knew deep in my bones that choosing monogamy out of fear and a desire for security wouldn't get us very far. I knew, even if they didn't, that couple entanglements only made the whole process of family building more drawn out and difficult, and I wasn't about to go down that road again.

It's uncomfortable to be on either side of this struggle. The truth is that we all have conflicting desires for inclusivity and exclusivity. When we become polarized on the monogamy issue we find ourselves distorting the reality of our complex emotions for the sake of a purist mentality. Knowing that my reputation might lead people to believe that I was rigidly polyamorous, I worked hard at keeping an open mind about monogamy. I've never met anyone I found totally fulfilling on every level, I would say, and I doubt that such a one exists. Don't take it personally. I'm a multidimensional person and I'm attracted to different qualities in different people. The more my heart opens, the more people I feel love for. If I ever feel moved to chose to be monogamous, I will, but not because someone insists upon it.

So why was I attracting lovers who ended up demanding monogamy? I didn't know but I knew I'd better find out because the whole process was very painful and certainly took all the fun out of polyamory. I began to ask myself hard questions. Was my own deeply conditioned desire for a white knight who would solve all my problems and take care of me forever sending out mating calls? At one of my own workshops I vowed to let go of this complex. Was I getting involved with too many lovers and needing some external constraints to narrow my focus? I decided to pay more attention to my own priorities. Was I simply coming up against cultural patterns that wouldn't disappear just because I challenged them? If so, how could I expect anyone else to break through centuries of conditioning when I couldn't do it myself? Without the support of my intimate network and the larger polyamorous community I've been building over the years, I'm sure I would have given up at this point. Instead, I realized that I needed to once again let go and allow the process to unfold in its own way.

And so began another cycle of deeper connections with old intimate friends and the appearance of delightful new additions to my ever growing family. I continue to pray for the strength, wisdom, humor, and clarity to take up permanent residence in the space of love which is really what my life is all about.

PATTERNS

We don't have information yet on sufficient numbers of people to say with certainty how most people build their families, but these are some of the patterns we've observed. I offer them to you as suggestions, not as absolutes.

Two plus two equals three. It's very rare for three or more single people to bond with each other all at the same time. And a single person is often reluctant to become the odd-one-out with a couple. But many stable triads that we know of, like the one described above, formed when two couples got together and then one couple broke up with one person going off separately.

Twelve divided by two equals two. Another common occurrence is for an intimate network of mixed couples and singles to end up with many of the singles coupled with each other and some of the couples uncoupled. We don't know of any intimate networks that have transformed into group marriages, but it is common for people to end up trading partners.

Three plus one equals three. Threesomes just don't seem to want to expand into foursomes. This holds true especially when adding a baby to a triad. This is not to say you can't do it, but it can be rocky, especially if there are unresolved issues about biological parentage.

Into the bed and out of the relationship. Leaping into bed with prospective family or network members may seem like a good way to get things started, but it usually isn't if you're interested in a long-term relationship. The reason is that in a group of people you're likely to find some bonds heating up before others. If you wait until everyone feels ready to proceed, you're much more likely to stay in balance.

Out of the bed and out of the relationship. It's also possible to err on the side of caution and be so hesitant about getting sexual prematurely that the natural flow of intimacy is effectively squashed. Once this happens it can be very hard to overcome the aura of celibacy or disinterest.

Shopping lists are toilet paper. It's become popular in some circles to compare shopping lists or social contracts as a way of screening potential partners. While comparing values and lifestyles is undoubtedly important, the reality is that most of us aren't totally conscious about who we are and what we want and need—especially in the unfamiliar territory of responsible nonmonogamy. This is why so many matches work only on paper and not in person. It's not unusual for people to end up with partners who are the exact opposite of what they said they wanted.

If A=B and A=C, B does not necessarily equal C. This is another case of real life refusing to conform to theory. As much as we would like the people we love to love each other, often they do not. You may chose to expect a miracle, but don't count on all your lovers understanding what you see in the others.

Same gender relationships are all powerful. Whether you are gay, straight, bisexual or don't know, you need to recognize that the quality of your family life will be determined by the quality of the same gender bonding. This bonding can express itself in many ways, so long as it occurs. If homophobia is allowed to remain an unexamined shadow issue, it may well sabotage your best efforts. Even where homophobia is not an issue, same gender bonding can be very delicate and needs sensitive care and nurturing.

ENJOY THE PROCESS

As I said earlier, building a multimate family or a stable intimate network can be a complicated undertaking. I've met many a seasoned veteran who has been working on it for several decades and who has grown discouraged by their failure to create a sustainable expanded family. I'm not always optimistic about the prospects myself, particularly when a promising relationship doesn't work out the way I had hoped it would and it looks like polyamory is the culprit. Here's what keeps me going.

First, I find the process itself to be a source of inspiration, growth and never ending surprises. For me, the joy of knowing that I have honored my own heart by staying open to the flow of love even when it doesn't bring me what I think I want is central to my well being. Staying in integrity with my values and my true feelings makes it all worthwhile.

My other source of energy is the realization that I am not dealing with a purely personal problem. Multimate families are rare in our culture, and we have as yet virtually no social institutions which support people in coming together in this way. Our difficulties are compounded by the fact that most polyamorous people fear ostracism or worse if they come out of the closet. Add to that centuries of conditioning which works against sharing sexual partners, not to mention other resources, and rampant emotional illiteracy and it's apparent that we're up against a lot of obstacles. But polyamory has enormous potential for weaving a new social fabric at a time when the old one has worn thin.

Hardly a day goes by now that I don't see some small but tangible evidence that my ongoing work to help make multimate families a legitimate option is having an impact. In fact it's now rippled out to the point where I know that other people will keeping it moving into ever-widening circles regardless of what I do myself. These little victories may not benefit me directly, but ultimately we will all be blessed by their fruits.

Chapter 10

03

POLYAMORY IN MYTH, ARCHETYPES AND HUMAN EVOLUTION

"We see Nature combining molecules and cells in the living body to construct separate individuals, and the same Nature, stubbornly pursuing the same course but on a higher level, combining individuals in social organisms to obtain a higher order of psychic results."
Pierre Teilhard de Chardin, *The Future of Man*

Our culture places such a strong emphasis on monogamy as the only natural way for humans to relate that we tend to ignore evidence which suggests that people around the globe and throughout history had no such prejudice.

The couple or dyad may be the quintessential unit for sexual reproduction, though even this is put into question by contemporary studies of mammalian breeding behaviors and recent advances in reproductive technology which allow single women or infertile couples to mix and match viable sperm and egg cells. But as our expectations for family life shift from the bare essentials of producing offspring to fulfilling the myriad psychological and spiritual needs of highly developed human beings, the twosome quickly loses its primacy.

There is something very special, very romantic, about the notion of two starry-eyed lovers locked in a close embrace. There is a yearning in our hearts for union with a twin soul or soul mate. But there is also a protean longing, deep within us, for a close-knit family of spiritual partners. We yearn, too, for the balance of the triangle, the eternal triangle which does not have to be a blueprint for tragedy, any more than the story of Romeo and Juliet has to be an index to the tragic fate of couples. And there is something very special about the symmetry of the square, the completeness of the four elements, the four directions, the four that is twice two. There is something special about every number, and in the natural world, combinations and subgroupings of various sizes all have their unique properties and their unique places in the overall picture.

By limiting marriage to two partners, we risk irreparable damage to fragile human ecosystems which thrive on diversity and complexity. Conversely, a variety of relationship niches allows everyone to find a place which fits their individual needs and desires. This kind of diversity is the hallmark of the natural world. In chemistry, elements are classified according to the number and type of bonds they will form. The polyamorous carbon molecule would be completely out of place in an exclusively pair-bonded world.

THE TRINITY

As pervasive as the image of two opposite-sex partners is in our culture's vision of perfect love and marriage, the number three is mythically even more basic in a universal sense. Two is the essence of a dualistic world view, but three is the number of synthesis. Three is what makes the world go round—harmoniously.

In every atom we find the proton or positive force, the electron or negative force and the neutron or synthesizing force. In music, a chord of three notes is more dynamic and powerful than one composed of only two notes. The triangle was emphasized as the basic unit by Dr. Roberto Assagioli[1], founder of psychosynthesis, who combined Western psychoanalytic knowledge with the metaphysical teachings of Alice Bailey. Buckminster Fuller[2], the design genius who created the geodesic dome, also focused on the triangle, pointing out that it is the only self-stabilizing, constant pattern in the Universe. Thus it is the basis of all structural systems.

Perhaps the most striking example of the primacy of the triad can be seen in the cultural icon of the Holy Trinity—the Father, the Son and the Holy Ghost or Spirit. And it seems quite obvious to me that the original Holy Trinity must have included not only the father and the child, but also the Great Mother. The substitution of the genderless Holy Ghost for the female principle was one of many systematic changes imposed upon a pre-existing culture by patriarchal Judeo-Christian clergy as they molded a new mythology for our present day society.

But to the extent that males take on the role of father and actively participate in rearing their offspring, humans are exposed to a basic family unit of three. The infant bonds not only with the mother but also with the father. Each one of us imprints upon at least two, not just one, significant other. The nature of these first nurturing relationships has great influence upon all subsequent ones.

This early patterning may explain why family systems pioneers such as Dr. Murray Bowen have found that the triangle is the basic emotional molecule[3]. Any emotional system can best be understood as a series of interlocking triangles. This is because a two person system is inherently unstable. Where there is one bond linking two people, this sole bond must absorb any tensions between the two. When it snaps, the connection is broken. In a three person system there are three bonds. So the triad is potentially three times as durable. One bond can break without completely destroying the whole system, allowing time for repairs or re-negotiation. If the bonds are of equal strength and flexibility, each one carries one third of the stress, thus distributing the load and making the whole relationship more durable. This is why the triangle is the basis of structural design in engineering. In the nuclear family a child is often pressed into service to balance the energies of the two parents. But another adult is far more appropriate for this role.

The usual portrayal of love triangles in our culture depicts strife, jealousy and betrayal. This viewpoint is no doubt related to Greek and Roman mythology in which amoral gods and goddesses are forever cheating on their partners and hatching horrific plots for revenge. Another example of this phenomenon is Freud's interpretation of the Oedipus myth, in which the hero murders his father and marries his mother, as the basis for all manner of psychosexual disorders. According to Freud, every child secretly aims for exclusive possession of his or her opposite-sex parent and jealously strives to eliminate the competition, the third leg of the triangle, the same-sex parent.[4]

But esoteric writings from many sources stress the balancing qualities of the third force[5].   Without the synthesizing energies of the third, we are left alternating between two irreconcilable polarities. For example, we have the state of excitement on the one hand and depression, its opposite, on the other. The synthesis of or balance between these two is a third quality called calm or serenity. In many traditions, the archetype of the eternal triangle is associated with the feminine. The inverted triangle is a universal symbol for the yoni or vagina. In Hindu and Buddhist mythology, happy triads are common. Clearly, the universal archetype of the love triangle is not inherently one of jealous struggle. It is up to us to select or create a mythology to live by which heals, not hurts.

THE SECRET DALLIANCE

One example of a healing mythology is found in the legends of the Secret Dalliance, which is the ancient Chinese term for sexual practices which extended beyond the couple[6]. Such practices were viewed as a legitimate means of stimulating potent, even magical, powers in both men and women throughout Asia. Multiple partner sex was also believed to rejuvenate the participants and promote longevity.

Knowledge of the sexual techniques associated with the Secret Dalliance was carefully guarded in the days of the great dynasties to enable the ruling classes to maintain their power over the common people. A man who spent himself with his first woman would be unable to satisfy the rest, so these techniques were very necessary in China where three to twelve wives were the norm for the relatively large middle class.

In India, the tantric Union of Three[7] was believed to release energies more powerful and potentially more dangerous than those experienced by a couple.   Texts offering special techniques for the proper channeling of these high-voltage energies warn against proceeding unless jealousy and egotism are absent.   Again, this knowledge was the province of adepts and nobles, and was deliberately kept from the lower classes. Perhaps the sentiment that triadic relationships were not suitable for the masses partly explains why these kinds of relationships are considered so unacceptable in today's democratic West.

Surviving Taoist and tantric texts emphasize the love-making of one man with two or more women, but it's likely that these reflect the imposition of a patriarchal culture on the earlier goddess-centered one where both men and women enjoyed multiple partners. For example, tablets dating from about 2300 BC which describe "reforms" in ancient Sumer (now southern Iraq) known as the reforms of Urukagina state that "women of former days used to take two husbands but the women of today would be stoned with stones if they did this," according to Merlin Stone in *When God Was A Woman*.[8]

There is also evidence that polyandry has been practiced in the Himalayan foothills. The great Indian epic, the Mahabharata, speaks of Queen Kunti and her many husbands and has as its heroes five brothers who were all married to the same woman. Even today, there are reports of women with more than one husband in Tibet and Ceylon.

POLYAMOROUS ARCHETYPES

Polytheistic cultures around the world, including Native American, African and Celtic cultures, have also honored the power of sexualove and lack the modern Judeo-Christian obsession with monogamy. It is beyond the scope of this book to explore all of these traditions, but brief mention of a few specifics will suggest the dramatically different perspective on polyamory found in other cultures.

For example, Native American teacher Harley Swiftdeer describes the talent for sexualove as a special gift, similar to a gift for music or for athletic ability. Such a gift may be chosen as a person's giveaway, or contribution to society. This lover archetype is very different from our culture's image of the driven nymphomaniac or the irresponsible Dionysian lady's man. Furthermore, the Native American archetype of the healer encompasses the use of an abundant erotic energy for healing. A similar archetype is known in Tibetan mythology as Sky Walking Woman. She is the free spirit who will not be possessed by any individual but whose life energy has the power to revitalize those who become intimate with her.

In the West, the most pervasive polyamorous archetype is Aphrodite, Greek Goddess of Love and Beauty. To the Romans she was Venus. In earlier times she was known as Inanna, Astarte, Ishtar or Isis. The Hindus call her Parvati.

Jungian analyst Jean Shinoda Bolen[9] calls Aphrodite the alchemical goddess because she alone among the Greek gods and goddesses had transformational power. She was also unique in that, while she had more lovers than any other goddess in Greek myth, she was not victimized and never suffered from her numerous love affairs as did most of the other goddesses. Neither was she jealous or possessive. Unlike her counterparts, she was allowed freely to choose both her husband and her many lovers. Aphrodite inspired poetry, communication and creativity as well as love. She is still renowned for her powerful magnetism. A twentieth century woman who embodied this archetype was Isadora Duncan, the inventor of modern dance.

Aphrodite's liaison with Hermes, God of Communication (called Mercury by the Romans), produced the bisexual, androgynous Hermaphroditus. Her long-term union with Ares, God of War (Mars to the Romans), produced a daughter, Harmonia. Thus Love and War combined to give rise to Harmony.

AN EVOLUTIONARY PERSPECTIVE

Speculation about the mating habits of prehistoric humans as well as observation of present day nonhuman primates are other sources of data often called upon to validate our current conjugal practices.

It's interesting to note that most scholars don't bother to ask whether or not males prefer or will accept multiple mates. It's assumed that the male will gladly take on as many females as he can gain access to. The big question is always whether females will accept more than one male, or sometimes, whether her consorts are willing to share her with other males.

Despite the questionable but well-publicized explanatory fictions invented by some culture-bound sociobiologists which treat monogamy as an evolutionary mandate, the weight of evidence suggests that early humans were not monogamous.

Prominent evolutionary biologist Lynn Margulis[10] points out that the erect penis of the human male is about five times larger than that of a gorilla. Human testicles are also much larger than those of gorillas and orangutans. Among the great apes, only the wildly promiscuous chimpanzees have bigger testicles than humans. Why is this? Probably it is an evolutionary adaptation to *sperm competition.* Sperm competition exists if two or more males copulate with the same female within a period of days. The one with the largest, best timed, and deepest penetrating ejaculation will be most likely to impregnate her. Consequently, the genes for large penises and testicles are more likely to be passed on.

This theory is supported by the discovery that in species of monkeys and apes with the highest testes-to-body-weight ratios, the females often mate with many males. For example, with chimpanzees, a species which has one of the highest ratios, the troop is usually composed of genetically related males who hunt together and who are willing to sexually share rather than exclusively possess a female. And female chimps in heat are inclined to encourage as many males to have a go as they can round up. This could be viewed as a precursor for early forms of group marriage, in which a group of related males bonded with a group of related females.

Further evidence cited by Margulis for the existence of sperm competition in humans is the discovery that men who know or suspect that their mate has not been monogamous actually produce more sperm and more semen than those who believe that their wives have no other lovers. Jealousy, she concludes, is an aphrodisiac.

But jealousy can also function to motivate other behaviors termed *sperm competition avoidance*. The huge gorilla with his one inch long erection and tiny testicles doesn't need a big penis to gain an evolutionary advantage. The alpha male simply prevents others from gaining access to the fertile females in his "harem." This pattern is more common in species where the male is significantly larger and more powerful than the female, a possible precursor for the form of polygamy practiced earlier by Biblical patriarchs and by patriarchs throughout the Arab world today.

Orangutans, who also have relatively tiny penises, are more likely to practice something called *take over avoidance*. That is, the mated pair remain alone and isolated in the jungle. Sperm competition is not an issue because there are no other contenders. One might see this idiosyncratic development, without pushing the extremes too far, as a possible precursor for our honeymoon custom and the exclusivity of the nuclear family.

Anthropologist Robert Smith[11] speculates that monogamous (take-over-avoidant or sperm-competition-avoidant) Homo sapiens may have been better fighters than their promiscuous well-hung (sperm competing) Homo erectus predecessors. Consequently, cooperative Homo erectus males, failing to protect their females from control by jealous and violent Homo sapiens, gradually disappeared.

Another perspective on evolutionary precedents for non-monogamous behavior can be found in the observations of anthropologist Sarah Blaffer Hrdy[12]. She points out that in primate species where the female mates with many different males, all the males in the troop are likely to be protective of her and her offspring. But in harem-type troops, males will kill nursing infants sired by another male. Thus we could speculate that men and women have different evolutionary agendas. The female's goal is to ensure the survival of all her offspring by enlisting the support of as many males as possible. The male's goal is to protect only those offspring which he knows to carry his genes and to eliminate all others. We might call this *post-natal sperm competition avoidance*. This could be viewed as a possible precursor for genocide.

THE BONOBO WAY

Perhaps the strongest evidence of a biological basis for polyamory comes from observations of the bonobo chimpanzee. Bonobos, also known as pygmy chimpanzees are only found in a small area of Zaire in central Africa and nothing was known about their behavior in the wild prior to the 1970's. At first they were confused with the common chimpanzee, but it turns out that bonobos, unlike common chimps, frequently copulate face-to-face and the females are sexually receptive throughout their ovulation cycle.[13] Observers agree that bonobos have a propensity for sharing sexual pleasure with a variety of partners independently of reproductive purposes.   In fact, genital play is used extensively both across and within genders as a means of bonding the group and defusing potential confrontations.

Male bonobos may use sex to reconcile with each other after an aggressive encounter and females use sex to reinforce social ties or relieve tension.   Bonobo females also build powerful alliances with each other through sexual sharing, a strategy which is thought to explain the peaceful and egalitarian relations between bonobo males and females. Unlike other primate species, such as common chimpanzees or baboons, bonobo females aren't afraid of the males and live in mixed gender groups. Although the males are physically larger and stronger, they don't dominate the females sexually or in any other way.

This discussion of primate mating patterns should not be interpreted as support for the notion that human sexuality is merely an extension of our genetically determined animal natures. However, it should be apparent from this brief discussion that the argument that monogamy is the only "natural" form of bonding has little basis in the study of primate sexual behavior. Quite the contrary, since humans appear to have more in common with bonobos than any other species and bonobos are happily polyamorous.

POLYAMORY AND THE PRE/POST FALLACY

Transpersonal psychologist Ken Wilber[14] draws our attention to an error that many of us make when looking at the evolution of human consciousness. He observes that we confuse the undifferentiated consciousness typical of primitive peoples, young children and psychotics, with the transcendental unitive consciousness of the mystic or saint. In other words, we mistakenly equate the undeveloped state with the highly developed state which it superficially resembles.

This same error is prone to occur when we look at the mating behaviors and family structures of primates and early humans. Evolution tends to follow a spiral, repeating a cyclic pattern which constantly brings us back to the same place, but at a higher level. Consequently, group marriages in prehistoric times may resemble the group marriages of the twenty-first century in that they include the same number of partners. But the dynamics of the relationships are likely to be very different. Similarly, the image of polygamy as male-dominated harems of females has little in common with the voluntary multiple partner relationships men and women choose today. Nor does forced monogamy directly correspond with a conscious choice of limiting oneself to one life partner.

Polyamory is not a throw back to more primitive modes of sexual relating. Neither is cosmic consciousness a kind of schizophrenic regression. Instead, polyamory is a more advanced form of relationship for men and women who have already mastered the basics of intimacy and are prepared to evolve beyond the confines of the isolated and, perhaps anachronistic dyad.

THE NEXT STEP

The concept of the grex provides a good evolutionary model for the next step in the evolution of the family. Biologists find that some species respond to environmental threats to their survival by gathering into highly interdependent groupings. The grex, or bonded group, is able to thrive under conditions which would be fatal to isolated individuals or mating pairs. Using group synergy, it increases the efficiency with which the basic functions, such as the input and distribution of nutrients and the coordination of activities are performed. In the case of humans, grexes or multiadult families can enhance our ability to share essential items such as food, shelter and information while assisting in the creation of valuable products and services.

BARBARA'S LOVE SONG

When I fall in love with a new lover,
Without falling out of love with another,
Oh...It feels so good to me
The way we all can be

When a lover of mine
Falls in love again
I can feel so warm and then
The circle growing wide
With lots of love inside

And now I'm learning and growing
Instead of tying, binding and owning,
We pull each other high
Together we can fly

I have a feeling deep in my limbs
Strong and warm inside of me
As I walk with my child and my lovers and myself
And the flowers and earth and trees

And my friends reach out, it goes on and on
And soon there's a whole society
In love with all humanity
Is the vision that I see

Today I walked out by the sea
the waves of love washed over me
The circle growing wide
From the sand clear to the sky

Loving, sharing, growing and caring
It's gonna' save the world, don't you know it.
Loving, sharing, growing and caring
It's gonna' save the world, don't you know it.

We're starting it now
We can handle it ... We know how.
Loving, sharing, growing and caring
It's gonna' save the whole world.

Chapter 11

છ્ક

HOW POLYAMORY BENEFITS US ALL

> *"If W.H. Auden is correct when he observes that 'As a rule it was only the pleasure-haters who became unjust,' then only a civilization that fosters erotic celebration can usher in a new era of justice-making."*
>
> Matthew Fox, *Original Blessing*

Polyamory is much more than an alternative choice for those who can't or won't confine themselves to one partner. As we said earlier, it is not for the faint of heart, and it is certainly not an "easy out" for those who haven't the moral fiber to commit themselves totally to a single partner. But if you find that loving more than one person at a time is the right choice for you, and you are willing to accept the responsibility for exercising this choice, then you deserve to know that, contrary to what you may have been told, polyamory is not only good for you, it is good for the planet! Here's why you should be proud to be polyamorous.

First of all, by choosing polyamory, you are expressing a desire to become a more evolved person. Many people who were inspired by books like Robert Heinlein's *Stranger in a Strange Land* or Robert Rimmer's *Harrad Experiment* in the sixties thought creating a multimate relationship would be easy. Instead, twenty years of false starts and painful discoveries have taught them that polyamory exacts a price. The fact is that humans have many contradictory impulses that pull us in the direction of nonexclusive love and simultaneously push us in the direction of jealousy and possessiveness. These opposing forces must be reconciled before we are truly free to love.

By choosing a multiple partner relationship, you're placing yourself in the center of the cyclone, where you will have many opportunities to confront these opposing forces. You'll undoubtedly make many mistakes. And if you're able to learn from them, you will find that you've gotten the benefit of several lifetimes worth of experience in a relatively short time.

Once you get past the initial struggles, your personal evolution should really speed up. Intimate relationships at their best are a path to higher consciousness and greater self-knowledge, largely because of the valuable feedback—or mirroring effect—one receives from a beloved. Having more than one partner at a time not only increases the available quantity of feedback, it also makes it harder to blame your partner for the problems you might be creating in the relationship. In other words, multiple partners actually help you to become a more conscious person.

Because multiple partner relationships are inherently more complex and demanding than monogamous ones and because you choose to explore territory beyond the norms of our culture, you will discover that you're on a path which offers some valuable lessons. Lessons about loving yourself, about tolerance for diversity, about speaking from the heart and communicating clearly, about learning to trust an internal sense of rightness and to think for yourself rather than blindly relying on outside opinion are only a sampling of the lessons. These qualities are earmarks of an emotionally and spiritually mature person—the kind of person who makes a good parent, who can contribute to his or her community and who can help our crisis-ridden planet make the transition into the next century.

Second, polyamory helps create stable and nurturing families where children can develop in an atmosphere of love and security. With the modern nuclear family well on its way to extinction, we are faced with a question of critical importance: Who will mind the children? Neither two-career nor single-parent families offer children full-time, loving caretakers, and quality day care is both scarce and expensive. Even at its best, full time institutional care (including public schooling) cannot provide the individual attention, intimacy, flexibility and opportunity for solitude that children need to realize their potential. And even under optimal conditions, the nuclear family tends to breed an unhealthily intense dependency which contributes significantly to social problems such as domestic violence and adolescent rebellion. The reality is that more often than not serial monogamy presents children, as well as parents, with a stressfully discontinuous family life. Meanwhile, an entire generation is at risk.

Many people believe that nonmonogamy is harmful to children. But in the case of *responsible* nonmonogamy, nothing could be farther from the truth. Multiple adult families and committed intimate networks have the potential of providing children with additional nurturing adults who can meet their material, intellectual and emotional needs. In other words, the child is not losing the attention of his or her biological parent, he or she is gaining new aunts, uncles and adopted parents. Meanwhile the adults can share parenting, and experience less stress and less burnout without losing any of the rewards of family life. In a group of men and women, it's more likely that one or two adults will be willing and able to stay home and care for the family, or that each could be available one or two days a week. If one parent dies or becomes disabled, other family members can fill the gap. Children have *more* role models, *more* playmates, and *more* love in a group environment.

Some political groups claim to be concerned about protecting children and families but support policies which actually undermine the well being of children and parents. Their real agenda is to force women back into traditional sex roles in a futile effort to return to an idealized past that never existed. Polyamory offers genuine new hope for revitalizing our families by expanding their boundaries. We can't go back to the days of tribes and close-knit extended families, but we can go forward to create intentional families whose members are committed to raising healthy children.

Third,   polyamory   is   ecologically   responsible. Sexualoving partners are more likely than friends or neighbors   to   feel   comfortable   sharing   housing, transportation, appliances and other resources.   Even if partners don't live communally, they frequently share meals, help each other with household repairs and projects, and vacation together. This kind of cooperation helps provide a higher quality of life while reducing individual consumption. Multiple partners also help in the renewal of our devastated human ecology by creating a sense of community.

Polyamory provides a strong incentive for people to once again settle permanently in a bioregion and put down roots. Not only are individuals be loathe to leave the support of a valued expanded family or intimate network, but multiple wage earners can provide an economic cushion which allows family members to refuse employer-generated relocation.

Fourth, polyamory can help us adapt to an ever more complex and quickly changing world. Have you noticed that life seems to speed up more with every passing year? Are you inundated with more information than you can absorb and more choices than you can evaluate? Do you see new technologies becoming obsolete almost before you can implement them? Yes, the future is here, and trying to keep up can be stressful if not impossible for a single person or a couple. But a small group of loving and well-coordinated partners can divide up tasks that would overwhelm one or two people. Multiple partner relationships can be an antidote to future shock.

Fifth, polyamory can help men and women break out of dysfunctional sex roles and achieve more equal, sexually gratifying, and respectful relationships. Most of us have unconsciously absorbed our culture's messages about appropriate behavior for men and women and the proper demeanor for husbands and wives. Marriage as we know it today is based on patterns established in Biblical times governing men's ownership of women. According to cultural historian Reay Tannahill, throughout the ancient Near East a free woman was not much better off than a slave. She could be stoned to death for taking a lover, while men were allowed as many secondary wives or concubines as they could afford.

We may think that our modern society has left this cruel legacy behind, but remember that women in the United States of America have had the right to vote for less than one hundred years, that men still control most of the wealth in both industrialized and third world countries, that the medical profession denied the existence of G Spot (one of women's primary centers for sexual gratification) until 1974, and that abortion was illegal in the USA prior to 1970.

Polyamory helps bring men and women face to face with our early sex role conditioning and demands that we transcend it. It requires that men and women alike overcome our competitive programming and that we invent new ways of relating since we can no longer fall back on simply doing it the way mom and dad did it. It encourages bonding between same gender adults and it provides a context of greater flexibility in meeting our sexual needs.

Finally, polyamory can help create a world of peace and abundance where all of humanity recognizes itself as one family. Idealistic? Yes. Realistic? Also yes! Our exclusively monogamous culture enshrines jealousy and possessiveness. Instead of working to eliminate jealousy and possessiveness so that people can freely choose how they will mate, our civilization tends to establish cultural and moral barriers that eliminate legitimate alternative relationships. By drawing a line around the couple or the nuclear family and saying, in effect, "inside this circle we share love and selflessly look out for each other, but outside this circle we keep anyone and everyone from taking what is ours," we perpetuate a system in which artificial boundaries are valued more than natural affinities.

Because the family is the basic building block of the culture the nature of the family has major implications for society as whole. Polyamory breaks down cultural patterns of control, as well as ownership and property rights between persons, and by replacing them with a family milieu of unconditional love, trust and respect, provides an avenue to the creation of a more just and peaceful world. By changing the size, structure and emotional context of the family, we change the personalities of the children developing in these families.

Children learn by example. We cannot teach our children to share and to love one another when we jealously guard and covertly control our most precious possessions—our spouses. By making the boundaries of the family more flexible and more permeable to the outside world, we set the stage for a new world view in which we recognize our kinship with all of humanity.

CHAPTER NOTES

CHAPTER 1: WHAT IS POLYAMORY?
1. Helen Fisher, *The Anatomy of Love: The Natural History of Monogamy, Adultery, and Divorce,* New York: WW Norton, 1992.

CHAPTER 2: THE ETHICS OF POLYAMORY
1. 1. Helen Fisher, *The Anatomy of Love: The Natural History of Monogamy, Adultery, and Divorce.* New York: WW Norton, 1992.
2. Carter Heyward, *Touching Our Strength: The Erotic as Power and the Love of God.* San Francisco: Harper Collins, 1989.
3. Richard Sutphen, *Radical Spirituality,* Malibu: Valley of the Sun, 1995.

CHAPTER 4: EIGHT STEPS TO SUCCESSFUL POLYAMORY
1. Riane Eisler, *Sacred Pleasure,* San Francisco: Harper Collins, 1995.

CHAPTER 5: JEALOUSY AS GATEKEEPER
1. Meredith Small " What's Love Got to Do with It?" *Discover,* June 1992, pp46-51.
2. Daniel Goleman, *Emotional Intelligence,* New York: Bantam Books, 1995.
3. Gordon Clanton and Lynn G. Smith (eds), *Jealousy,* Englewood Cliffs, NJ: Prentice-Hall, 1977.
4. Robert A. Masters, *The Way of the Lover,* W. Vancouver, BC: Xanthyros Foundation, 1988.
5. Ron Mazur, *The New Intimacy: Open Marriage and Alternative Lifestyles,* Boston: Beacon Press, 1973.
6. Michael Sky, *Breathing: Expanding Your Power and Energy,* Santa Fe, NM: Bear & Company, 1990.

CHAPTER 8: FINDING YOUR TRIBE
1. Bertrand Russell, *Marriage and Morals,* New York: Bantam, 1959.

2. Dane Rudyar, *Directives for New Life*, Rail Road Flat, CA: Seed Publications, 1971.
3. Bhagwan Shree Rajneesh, *Sex*, Woodland Hills, CA: Lear Enterprises, 1981.
4. Robert and Anna Francoeur, *Hot and Cool Sex: Cultures in Conflict*, New York: Harcourt, Brace & Jovanovich, 1974.

CHAPTER 10: POLYAMORY IN MYTH, ARCHETYPES AND HUMAN EVOLUTION

1. Roberto Assagioli, *The Act of Will*, Baltimore, MD: Penguin, 1974.
2. Buckminster Fuller, *Synergetics*, New York: Macmillan, 1975.
3. Murray Bowen, *Family Therapy in Clinical Practice*, New York: Jason Aronson, 1982.
4. Sigmund Freud, *General Psychological Theory*, New York: Collier Books, 1963,
5. John G. Bennett, *Sex*, Sherbourne UK: Coombe Springs Press, 1975.
6. Nik Douglas, and Penny Slinger, *Sexual Secrets*, New York: Destiny Books, 1979.
7. *ibid.*
8. Merlin Stone, *When God Was a Woman*, New York: Harcourt, Brace, Jovanovich, 1976.
9. Jean Shinoda Bolen, *Goddesses in Every Woman*, San Francisco: Harper & Row, 1984.
10. Lynn Margulis and Dorion Sagan, Mystery Dance: *On the Evolution of Human Sexuality*, New York: Summit Books, 1991.
11. *ibid.*
12. Sarah Blaffer Hrdy "The Primate Origins of Human Sexuality," In *The Evolution of Sex*, edited by Robert Bellig and George Stevens, San Francisco: Harper & Row, 1988.
13. Meredith Small, "What's Love Got to Do with It?" *Discover*, June 1992, pp 46-51.
14. Ken Wilber, *The Atman Project*, Wheaton, IL: Theosophical Publishing House, 1980.

POLYAMORY IN BOOKS AND FILMS

The following bibliography of books and videos portraying polyamory as a viable option is by no means exhaustive, but it does include all those works that have shaped my own world view. Many of the older ones are out of print, but you should be able to obtain them via interlibrary loan if you can't locate a used copy. Try writing to the publisher for help as well. Let them know there's a market for books on polyamory out here!

NONFICTION

Beecher, J. and Bienvenu, R. **The Utopian Vision of Charles Fourier,** *Boston: Beacon Press, 1971*
Charles Fourier was so far ahead of his time that we still haven't caught up with him. Fascinating, if eccentric, account of his intuitive discovery of the laws of passionate attraction and his ideas about creating a harmonious society. Fourier believed that each person has a set capacity for the number of lovers s/he can integrate simultaneously, with a range from zero to eight.

Chapman, Audrey, **Man-Sharing: Dilemma or Choice,** *New York: William Morrow, 1987*
Chapman is not exactly a fan of nonmonogamy, but she is realistic enough to recognize that our society is already "bordering on polygamy" and she counsels women to face the facts and find ways to make it work for them. Making it work means taking an active role and becoming polyamorous themselves rather than passively accepting male infidelity.

Clanton, G. and Smith, L.G., **Jealousy,** *Englewood Cliffs: Prentice Hall, 1977*
Excellent anthology for those who find sexual jealousy to be the main obstacle to inclusive relationships. Contains both theoretical and practical perspectives with sections on the experience of jealousy, jealousy and culture, and managing jealousy.

Clanton, G. and Downing, C., **Face to Face to Face,** *New York: Dutton, 1975*
Diary-style account of a couple adding a third. Covers the rise and fall of the relationships from each person's viewpoint. Very instructive about what works and what doesn't. Also highlights the importance of the same-sex relationship in a triad.

Constantine, L. and J. **Group Marriage,** *New York: Collier Books, 1973*
Landmark study on group marriage by husband and wife team family therapists. Based on their in home visits with over thirty multilateral families, this is still the most comprehensive published research on the topic. Good coverage of the impact of group marriage on children.

Davis, Stephen and Royale, Lyssa, **Future Sex,** *Phoenix: Personal Enhancement Press, 1991*
The basic premise of this book is that we need to question our supposedly universal sexual assumptions. The bulk of the material consists of channeled interviews with extra-terrestrials about their sexual mores and practices, which turns out to be a good device for illustrating the diversity of possible attitudes. All of these "alien" ideas are actually represented on earth anyway, so don't let your skepticism turn you away. My favorite part of the book is the discussion of Stephen's and his wife Heide's own struggle to establish a healthy nonmonogamous relationship. Their use of the codependency paradigm to characterize monogamy as an addiction is particularly valuable.

Easton, Dossie and Liszt, Catherine, **The Ethical Slut,** *San Francisco: Greenery Press, 1997.*
A delightful new manual for men and women who want to live an open sexual lifestyle. According to the authors, an ethical slut is someone who dreams of freedom, sex, an abundance of friends, flirtation, and consensual conquest and who believes in living these dreams. Practical advice and frank firsthand confessions from the experienced buddy or big sister you probably weren't fortunate enough to have.

Eisler, Riane, **Sacred Pleasure: Sex, Myth, and the Politics of the Body,** *San Francisco: Harper, 1995*
Eisler offers a compellingly complete analysis of how our cultural attitudes toward love, sex, and family became so destructive as well as some clear guidelines for finding our way into a truly humane and sustainable future, where pleasure rather than pain is the basis for relationship with each other and with Earth. One key, says Eisler, is the restructuring of the family. This volume offers a political and philosophical basis for the polyamory movement with only a few direct references to the issue of enforced monogamy.

Francoeur, Robert, **Eve's New Rib,** *New York: Harcourt, Brace, & Jovanovich, 1972*
Explores the impact of technological and sociological change on the institution of marriage with an eye to Christian ethics. Written by a married Catholic priest who advocates "flexible monogamy" in which secondary sexual relationships are permitted.

Francoeur, Robert and Anna, **Hot and Cool Sex: Cultures in Conflict,** *New York: Harcourt, Brace & Jovanovich, 1974*
Billed as an examination of the changing sexual and marriage patterns in American society within a religious and historical context, this is a 70's version of *Love Without Limits.* Includes information on Oneida, Mormon polygamy, and the Sandstone Experiment as well as the previous generation of poly activists.

Fisher, Helen, **Anatomy of Love: The Natural History of Monogamy, Adultery, & Divorce,** New York: Norton, 1992
Fisher's basic premise is that life long sexual exclusivity is unnatural for humans as well as virtually all other animals. She speaks authoritatively, frequently citing animal behavior studies and statistics for support, but many of her conclusions are in fact highly speculative. While Fisher has done an excellent job of unmasking the typical behavior hiding beneath our cultural norms, her apparent disregard for evidence of bonding beyond the dyad is a serious flaw. Fisher's perspective on the evolution

of the family provides another interesting twist. She attributes modern family values to the agricultural tradition and views the current instability as a "return to our nomadic roots." Divorce, secret affairs, single parents, and blended families are nothing new, she asserts, and have always been common. The only new development, she insists, is single people living alone who *choose* a network of friends they consider family.

Friedman, Sonia, **Secret Loves: Women with Two Lives,** *New York: Crown, 1994*
A sympathetic look at women who have maintained long term secret love affairs while keeping their marriages intact. So much for the myth that women are naturally monogamous.

Friends and Lovers: Relationships in a Humane Sustainable Culture *Issue #10 (Summer 1985) of* In Context, *$15 from POB 11470, Bainbridge Island, WA 98110*
This issue was guest edited by the UV Family and contains their article, *The Possible Relationship,* which is probably the most illuminating piece to date on how—and why—multimate relationships work. This family has now been together for over 20 years and is more loving than ever! These folks know whereof they speak.

Heyn, Dalma: **The Erotic Silence of the American Wife,** *New York: Signet, 1992*
Brilliant, highly readable stories of why women stray from monogamy expose conventional marriage as a patriarchial misogynist institution. The message is that women's pleasure and eroticism is valid and important. Heyn urges women not to sell their sexuality out in order to fit the socially prescribed criteria for "good girls" and "perfect wives."

Heyward, Carter, **Touching Our Strength: The Erotic as Power and the Love of God,** *San Francisco: Harper, 1989*
This inspiring book on sexual justice by a lesbian Episcopal priest and professor of theology is a rich source for a sexual ethic that

truly honors diversity. Heyward's touchstone is the concept of mutual empowerment.

Johnson, Sonia, **The Ship that Sailed into the Living Room,**
Estancia, NM: Wildfire Books, 1991
The infamous former housewife who was excommunicated from the Mormon church for her feminist views explores the issue of how we can associate intimately with one another and be totally free. The monogamy/nonmonogamy issue, she concludes, is irrelevant from a true feminist perspective.

Kinkade, Kat, **Is It Utopia Yet?** *Louisa, VA: Twin Oaks Publishing, 1994*
A lively, engaging account of how an egalitarian intentional community has grown and changed over its twenty-five year lifespan. Twin Oaks was originally conceived in part as an experiment in implementing the concepts described in BF Skinner's *Walden Two*, but has since evolved in other directions. While reluctant to discuss sex, Kinkade admits that life-long monogamy has never been the norm at Twin Oaks and shares some pithy anecdotes about relationships there. A good example of how polyamory plays an important role in the larger intentional communities movement.

Karlen, Arno, **Threesomes: Studies in Sex, Power, And Intimacy,** *New York: William Morrow, 1990*
This author takes a dim view of triads, but this is one of the only books published in the last decade which even acknowledges that there are lifeforms beyond the couple. The style is pretty academic but the descriptions of threeway sex are graphic.

Klaw, Spencer, **Without Sin: The Life and Death of the Oneida Community,** *NY: Viking, 1993*
Most recent of many books on the famous early polyamorous Oneida community. Includes an account of founder John Humphrey Noyes system of complex marriage.

LaChapelle, Dolores, **Sacred Land, Sacred Sex: Rapture of the Deep**, Durango, CO: Kivaki Press, 1992
LaChapelle fully and flawlessly answers the critical question of why polyamory is more ecologically healthy than monogamy. Intended as a manual on deep ecology, this magnificent resource combines impeccable scholarship with a personal, readable style to create a straightforward analysis of what's wrong with our culture, how it got that way, and what to do about it. By illuminating the links between caring for the earth, natural birth control, and a poly lovestyle, we begin to see the importance of validating alternatives to monogamy.

Lano, Kevin and Claire Parry, **Breaking the Barriers to Desire**, Nottingham UK: 1995
The first British book to look at modern day polyamory, this volume is a collection of both personal and theoretical essays by writers from the UK, Australia, and the USA. Lots of firsthand information but small type and awkward writing create their own barriers.

Lawrence, Raymond, **The Poisoning of Eros: Sexual Values in Conflict**, New York: Augustine Moore Press, 1989. $21.50 postpaid from 432 W 47th St #2W, NY, NY 10036
This book traces the conflict between sex affirming and sex negating religious leaders from Greco-Roman times to the present day. Lawrence is a poly positive Episcopalian minister who offers a proposal for a new sexual ethic based on the affirmation of our sexuality and valuing "communitas" over exclusivity. His case is brilliantly argued and includes examples of prominent nonmonogamous modern day church leaders such as Karl Barth and Paul Tillich.

Libby, R. and Whitehurst, R,. **Marriage and Alternatives: Exploring Intimate Relationships**, Glenview, IL: Scott, Foresman, 1977
Textbook-style anthology is an excellent introduction to the subject of nonmonogamy. Includes chapters by most of the key thinkers in the first wave of the sexual revolution.

Lobell, J. and M., **John and Mimi: A Free Marriage** *New York: St. Martin's Press, 1972*
Sexually explicit and intelligent account of a couple's experiences with free love in the psychedelic era. Will make you long for the good old days.

Masters, Robert Augustus, **The Way of the Lover**
W. Vancouver, British Columbia: Xanthyros Foundation, 1988
A collection of short essays and poems by a modern spiritual teacher in the fourth way tradition. Masters is blunt, merciless and right on target in discussing how our culture's sexual mores inhibit growth and awakening. He covers jealousy, sex addiction, S&M, homosexuality, pornography, and, of course, enforced monogamy.

Mazur, R., **The New Intimacy: Open Marriages and Alternative Lifestyles,** *Boston: Beacon Press, 1973*
Unitarian minister offers some good advice, especially on coping with jealousy. Mazur's categories are extremely useful in discovering how jealousy personally impacts you.

Nearing, Ryam **The Polyfidelity Primer,** *(3rd Edition), Captain Cook, HI: PEP Publishing, 1992*
Loving More Magazine co-founder Ryam Nearing's handbook on polyfidelity is about as wholesome and non-threatening an introduction to the subject of group marriage as one could ever hope to find. Includes excellent sections on distinguishing (and choosing) among the different varieties of polyamory and on dealing with finances. The tone is practical and straightforward.

Posner, Richard, **Sex and Reason,** *Cambridge: Harvard Univ Press, 1992*
A very academic but fascinating compilation of research on sex from biology, religion, sociology, economics and other theoretical disciples which includes quite a bit on nonmonogamy. Posner is a judge and a legal scholar and his basic perspective is an economic/political one. His discussion of the 1878 Supreme Court ruling which outlawed polygamy in the USA concludes

that the point of monogamy is to permit political power to be concentrated in the state.

Ramey, James, **Intimate Friendships,** *Englewood Cliffs, N.J.: Prentice Hall, 1976*
The best of the first wave books on responsible nonmonogamy. It's a thoughtful look at how changing values and lifestyles point to new models for relationships with useful information on how to evaluate some of these innovations. The future Ramey describes is still on the horizon and the book is quite current.

Rimmer, Robert, **Let's Really Make Love: Sex, the Family, and Education in the Twenty-first Century,** *Amherst NY: Prometheus, 1995.*
The latest non-fiction work from the author of the *Harrad Experiment* is more about sexual politics than polyamory. However it does provide a valuable historical perspective on the modern polyamory movement.

Rogers, Carl, **Becoming Partners: Marriage and Its Alternatives,** *N.Y.: Delacourte Press, 1972*
The famous empathic, nondirective therapist at his best. Rogers predicts that by the year 2000 the attitude of possessiveness in marriage will be greatly diminished. The case histories which make up most of the book include many experiments with nonmonogamy. Rogers probes his interviewees with an impeccable nonjudgemental stance.

Rudhyar, Dane, **Directives for New Life,** *Rail Road Flat, CA: Seed Publications, 1971*
This wonderful little book is a clear and simple prescription for creating a sane society. Rudhyar sees the interpersonal factor as the key to social change and recommends polyvalent relationships based on inclusive, unpossessive love. His concept of the seed group sums up the spiritual basis for polyamory.

Russell, Bertrand, **Marriage and Morals,** *New York: Bantam, 1959*
First published in 1929; a genuine classic by the Nobel Laureate.
An entertaining and exquisitely clear critique of monogamy.

Seligson, Marcia, **Options,** *N.Y.: Grosset & Dunlap, 1977*
A journalist's somewhat sensational account of her investigation
of alternatives to monogamy. Frank and funny.

Singer, June, **Energies of Love: Sexuality Revisioned** *Garden
City: Doubleday, 1983*
Marvelous, beautifully written theoretical work, placing inclusive
relationships in a psychological and spiritual context.

Talese, Gay, **Thy Neighbor's Wife,** *New York: Doubleday, 1980*
Another journalist's adventures. Covers the rise and fall of the
notorious Sandstone experiment.

Tessina, Tina, **Love Styles: How to Celebrate Your Differences**
Hollywood: Newcastle Pub., 1987
A "how-to" book of exercises and examples with an emphasis on
alternatives to traditional relationships. Also includes stories of
several nonmonogamous domestic pioneers.

Thamm, Robert, **Beyond Marriage and the Nuclear Family** *San
Francisco: Canfield, 1975*
A behaviorist college professor's somewhat intellectual account
of his investigation of alternatives to monogamy. The book
accompanied an experiment in communal living which lasted for
seven years.

West, Celeste, **Lesbian Polyfidelity,** *San Francisco: Booklegger
Publishing, 1996*
Celeste West has written a wise, witty, and charming manual for
all polyamorous people (she uses polyfidelity to mean
polyamory). Based on a survey of 500 lesbians, the ring of
authenticity comes through in the nitty gritty detail of the
personal stories related here.

FICTION

Alexander, Thea, **2150 A.D.** *New York: Warner Books, 1976*
Inspiring utopian fantasy about a society where jealousy and
possessiveness do not exist. An underground classic despite the
lack of literary finesse.

Bishop, Conrad and Fuller, Elizabeth, **Loveplay,** *Philadelphia:
WordWorks, 1993. $10 from 115 Arch St, Philadelphia, PA 19106*
An original two act play in which polyamory is part of a rich mix
of sexual and emotional challenges faced by some very true to life
contemporary characters.

Bradley, Marion Zimmer, **The Forbidden Tower,** *New York:
DAW Books, Inc., 1977*
Low-tech science fiction tale about a race of telepaths with sexual
mores similar to, but slightly different from, those of earthlings.
Twin sisters and their new husbands find themselves forming a
powerful foursome which becomes the core of a new culture.
Bradley (best known for *The Mists of Avalon*) has captured the
essence of multipartner lovemaking in this volume of the popular
Darkover novels.

Callenbach, Ernest, **Ecotopia** and **Ecotopia Emerging,** *New York:
Bantam, 1975*
Two more underground classics, packed with information about
ALL aspects of life in a sustainable, ecological utopia where
people are not phobic about multiple intimate relationships.

Dyer, Wayne, **Gifts from Eykis,** *New York: Pocket Books, 1984*
Amusing and uplifting allegory on new paradigm love with useful
input on dealing with negative emotions, such as guilt, fear,
jealousy and dependency. Also provides encouragement for
challenging the status quo and realizing utopian dreams.

Heinlein, Robert, **Stranger in a Strange Land,** *New York: Berkeley, 1961*
Grandaddy of the underground classics; often credited with beginning the modern alternative lifestyle movement. Recently reissued in an unexpurgated edition. If you can overlook what would now be considered sexist dialogue, you're left with a grand vision of sexualoving religious communities.

Heinlein, Robert, **The Moon Is a Harsh Mistress,** *New York: Berkeley, 1968*
Another Heinlein classic, which introduces the concept of line marriage.

Kingsbury, Donald, **Courtship Rite,** *New York: Simon & Schuster, 1982*
Science fiction adventure about a society where a six-person marriage is considered the ultimate achievement.

Piercy, Marge, **Woman on the Edge of Time,** *New York: Fawcett Crest, 1976*
Better written but more depressing than any of the above, this feminist utopia has a lot in common with the more patriarchal visions above—i.e., nonexclusive relationships and expanded family.

Lessing, Doris, **The Marriages Between Zones Three, Four, and Five,** *New York: Alfred A. Knopf, 1980*
Doris Lessing has been teaching us about relationships—and other important matters—through her novels for several decades. In this parable, the female ruler of a highly evolved society where multiadult families are the norm is sent to mate with the male ruler of a backward, violent and repressive patriarchal kingdom.

Rimmer, Robert, **The Harrad Experiment, Proposition 31, Thursday My Love, The Rebellion of Yale Marratt, Love Me Tomorrow, The Love Exchange** *(and more!). New York: Signet*
Robert Rimmer has done a more thorough job of mapping the territory of inclusive relationships than anyone. *Rebellion of Yale Marratt* and *Love Me Tomorrow* are my personal favorites because they mix spiritual, ceremonial sex into the brew. A twenty-fifth anniversary edition of *Harrad Experiment* is still in print.

Rimmer, Robert, **The Immoral Reverend***, Amherst, NY: Prometheus, 1985*
One of Rimmer's best and most recent novels tells the story of the founding of a new religion which embraces erotic love and polyamory. I can't wait till this one comes into manifestation.

Robinson, Spider and Jeanne, **Stardance***, New York: Dial Press, 1979*
Perhaps the most inspiring and most contemporary of all polyamorous science fiction, this blend of bio- social eco-consciousness is too good to miss. The fast moving plot revolves around the founding of the first zero-gravity, off planet dance troupe and the subsequent use of dance as a medium to communicate with some very exotic extra-terrestrials. It turns out that the personality characteristics required to dance in zero gravity are remarkably similar to those needed for polyamory, and guess what? The world's first weightless dance company evolves into a transparently intimate and synergistic group marriage on their way to making a genuine evolutionary leap.

Starhawk, **The Fifth Sacred Thing***, New York: Bantam, 1993*
A delightful tale of a self-sufficient, spiritually and ecologically responsible culture struggling to preserve itself from the attacks of an evil empire. Imagine that the best and highest elements of the neopagan movement have become cultural norms and you'll have a glimpse of Starhawk's vision. A vision with polylove and expanded family at its heart.

Varley, John, **The Persistence of Vision,** *New York: Dell, 1978*
A tantric teacher gave me a xerox copy of this sensual fantasy
over a decade ago and it left a deep and lasting impression. You
too will be inspired by this delightful story by one of our best sci
fi authors of a community of blind and deaf people who
communicate via whole body touch. To them, sex is literally
conversation.

Walker, Alice, **The Temple of My Familiar,** *NY: Harcourt Brace
Jovanovich, 1989*
Best selling novel by one of the most talented Americans writing
today. Most reviewers have neglected to mention that the book's
main characters engage in multimate relationships which are for
the most part portrayed in a positive light.

FEATURE FILMS

Carrington (1995)
The talented Emma Thompson stars in this moving portrayal of
bohemian expanded family in post war England. Thompson
portrays a young tomboyish artist who falls in love with a
homosexual writer. The couple are completely devoted to each
other but their incompatible sexual orientations require them to
include their respective lovers into the family.

Cesar and Rosalie (1972)
In French with English subtitles, starring Yves Montand, Romy
Schneider and Sami Frey. Rosalie is a divorced single parent who
maintains a friendship with her starving artist ex after becoming
romantically involved with Cesar, a successful businessman. But
things get really interesting when her first love, who is now a
famous cartoonist, returns to town. Rosalie stubbornly refuses
to choose one man over the other, but Cesar becomes so jealous
he eventually drives Rosalie to run away with her other lover.
Finally Cesar sees the light, and all three try to make a go of it.
So far so good, but Rosalie can't handle this much love and runs
away with her daughter leaving the two men to console each
other.

French Twist (1996)
Starring Victoria Abril and Josianne Balasko. A rare film which is poly-positive right through to the end. This touchingly realistic comedy is about a married couple whose pleasant life in the south of France is transformed when a goddess-adorned van driven by a disco DJ dyke named Marijo breaks down in front of their home. Marijo soon becomes the wife's lover and the philandering husband struggles to come to terms with polyamory.

Jules and Jim (1962)
Directed by Francois Truffaut and starring Jeanne Moreau, Oskar Werner and Henry Serre. One of the first feature films to address the dynamics of inclusive relationships, it's a moving drama and well worth seeing even though it doesn't exactly make you want to run right out and join a triad. It's the story of two good friends who find both joy and tragedy loving the same woman.

Heartbeat
Starring Nick Nolte. The touching story of famous beat writer Jack Kerouac's three-way relationship with the infamous Neal Cassady and Neal's wife, Carolyn. Wonderful scenes of another kind of life behind the facade of a suburban tract house.

My Other Husband (1985)
French film with English subtitles, starring Miou Miou. It's a wonderfully funny and upbeat look at how bigamy can be a natural and reasonable solution to a sticky situation. Miou Miou accidentally finds herself running secretly between two separate families. Finally the deception is exposed and after a few protests, the two husbands become fond of each other. This time triadic domestic bliss ends with the death of one of the husbands from a sudden heart attack. Are we getting warmer?

Micki and Maude (1984)
Hollywood comedy starring Dudley Moore, Amy Irving and Donna Reinking as three unintentional polygamists. Some funny if predictable scenes about close brushes with exposure as

Dudley's two wives give birth at the same time in the same
hospital as he frantically tries to be in two places at once. Most
of the film focuses on the farcical aspects of the cheating
husband and the awkward efforts of the women to resolve the
situation, but the tone is basically positive and everyone lives
happily ever after. The final scenes show the two women happily
advancing in their careers as Dudley joyously tends their half-
dozen children. A good one for introducing children to the
concept of polyamory.

Paint Your Wagon (1969)
Film version of the Broadway musical starring Lee Marvin, Jean
Seberg and Clint Eastwood. Surprisingly, this otherwise ordinary
Western about the California gold rush has Marvin and
Eastwood coping with the shortage of women by happily sharing
a wife.

Threesome (1994)
A college housing crunch finds two boys and a girl sharing a
dorm suite. The jock is turned on by the girl, the girl by the
"sensitive" guy, the sensitive guy by the jock. Eventually they all
end up in bed together and share some blissful triadic moments
before caving in to social pressure to go straight.

Summer Lovers (1982)
Daryl Hannah stars in this romance about a young couple
vacationing on a Greek island who have an affair with a French
woman. Instead of the usual complications and uproar, a good
time is had by all. A beautiful film.

ORGANIZATIONAL DIRECTORY

Church of All Worlds
POB 1542
Ukiah, CA 95482
This neopagan group was founded in 1962 by Oberon Zell with inspiration from Heinlein's Stranger in a Strange Land. Based in Northern California with local "nests" all over the United States and abroad, CAW has created a culture in which polyamorous relationships are pretty much the norm and jealousy is considered neither necessary nor desirable. This group also publishes *Green Egg Magazine*.

Delaware Valley Synergy
POB 1551
Bensalem, PA 19020
DVS was founded in 1975 as an offshoot of the Los Angeles Family Synergy group inspired by Robert Rimmer's writings. Their goal is to provide a supportive and encouraging environment for people exploring open relationships in the Delaware Valley. Many of the original members are still involved. They host a variety of rap groups, social events, and sexually permissive parties for members and publish a monthly newsletter.

Family Tree
POB 441275
Somerville, MA 02144
This is another Rimmer inspired group which has been around since the early seventies. Joan Constantine, co-author of the classic *Group Marriage* edits a monthly newsletter which provides information on upcoming FT events, reports on milestones in members lives, and discusses issues in open relating. Their mission is to contribute to an increased understanding and acceptance of alternative lifestyles. A core of long time members creates a base for this Boston area polyamorous network.

Family Synergy
POB 3073
Huntington Beach, CA 92605
Family Synergy describes itself as a nonprofit, volunteer-run educational organization for people interested in nonpossessive, caring relationships. They publish a monthly newsletter and sponsor an annual conference each summer. Based in Los Angeles, this group has also been around since the early seventies and has had trouble attracting younger (under 50) members.

Liberated Christians
POB 32835
Phoenix, AZ 85064
A support group for Christians who want to love more. More sexuality oriented than most polyamory groups, these folks are dedicated to overcoming sex negative conditioning and sponsor regular events toward that end. They publish a very chatty newsletter.

Live the Dream
6454 Van Nuys Blvd
Van Nuys, CA 91401. 818/361-6737
LTD split off from Family Synergy some years back and has a strong neopagan, sci fi flavor. Founder Terry Brussel-Gibbons and her partners publish a monthly events calendar and hold regular meetings in the Los Angeles area.

♥Loving More
POB 4358
Boulder, CO 80306. 800/424-9561 ryam@lovemore.com
Loving More was formed in 1994 when Deborah Anapol's IntiNet and Ryam Nearing's Polyfidelitous Educational Productions merged to form ALI. Deborah left in 1996 to create the Sacred Space Institute and Loving More is now run by Ryam Nearing and family. They publish the quarterly *Loving More Magazine* and hold an annual conference. Members come from all over the USA and internationally. They also hold monthly potluck/discussion groups in Boulder.

Network for a New Culture
510/538-0369
jonrsl@aol.com
NFNC is a national network inspired by the German Free Love community called ZEGG whose philosophy is that love and sex are essential parts of our being so people must be free to follow their hearts in both short term and long term relationships. For the past couple of years they have held summer and winter "camps" where people can experience community for a few days and where one-on-one sexual adventures are encouraged. You can view their website at http:\\www.loveandcommunity.com.

Pali Paths
POB 22586
Honolulu, HI 96823. 808/239-6824
Polyamory support group meets weekly in Honolulu. Members receive a monthly events calendar.

Potomac Area Polyamory Network
POB 8162
Silver Spring, MD 20907. 301/587-0514
Washington, D.C. area support group for polyamorous people. They hold monthly meetings and publish a newsletter.

♥Sacred Space Institute
POB 4322
San Rafael, CA 94913 415/507-1739 pad@well.com
The Sacred Space Institute is a division of IntiNet Resource Center which offers workshops and individualized consultation on polyamory, new paradigm relating, sexual healing and sacred sexuality all over the USA and internationally. Workshops are facilitated by Dr. Deborah Anapol and a variety of friends and lovers. The annual conference celebrates diversity in lovestyles and promotes the union of sex and spirit. Check out their website at **http:\\www.lovewithoutlimits.com** for current information on upcoming events and publications.

Touchpoint
POB 408
Chloride, AZ 86431
Stan Major publishes this quarterly newsletter which offers a
national listing of personal ads for polyamorous people as well as
other resource listings.

*Please note that while all of the groups above support people exploring
polyamory,* none of these organizations are swing clubs. *If you are
interested in swinging, try contacting:*

The Lifestyles Organization (TLO)
2641 W. LaPalma Ave.
Anaheim, CA 92801   714/821-9953
Founded in 1973 by Robert and Geri McGinley, this is the group
that sponsors the Lifestyles Convention, a huge annual gathering
for "playcouples" currently held in San Diego, California. They
also sponsor tropical vacation tours and other social events in
Southern California. Their NASCA division publishes a
directory of North American swing clubs.

ONLINE RESOURCES

WEBSITES

http:\ \ www.lovewithoutlimits.com
The *Love Without Limits* website offers an opportunity for all
those making the shift to new paradigm relating to find out about
upcoming events, publications, and the latest developments on
the domestic frontier. Tune in for inspiration, support, and up
to date information from Dr. Deborah Anapol and Friends.

http:\ \ www.lovemore.com
Loving More Magazine website includes a chatsite and email list as
well as events calendars, electronic books and articles, and
membership information. They plan to make all back issues
available soon. You can also find links to related sites.

EMAIL LISTS
An email list is like a giant phone tree which automatically circulates email messages to and from everyone on the list.

Poly email list
Formerly the "triples mailing list." The content ranges from sticky situations encountered by polyamorists to reviews of relevant books, conferences, and media as well as varied off-topic musings. If you're feeling isolated and don't mind having your mailbox flooded with messages, you'll love it. To subscribe send a message to:

owner-poly@lupine.org

This list is the oldest and probably the biggest, but many providers such as AOL now have their own poly lists and conferences.

Poly-Activism email list
This list is specifically for people interested in taking action intended to counteract the political, social, and religious enforcement of monogamy as the only acceptable type of relationship. It includes announcements and discussion of events and situations which promote greater awareness of polyamory as a legitimate option for intimate relating. To subscribe send email to: majordomo@world.std.com with the following line in the body of the message (only): subscribe poly-activism

NEWSGROUPS
Unlike the email lists, the newsgroups do not send messages to you. Instead, they compile comments from participants which you can read at your leisure.

alt.polyamory
Alt.polyamory is for discussion of poly related topics. The content is similar to that of the poly email list. There are many swinger sites on the internet but this is not one of them.

alt.poly.personals
Personal ads and other overt efforts to connect with potential partners are not permitted in alt.polyamory. Instead they belong here.

GLOSSARY

Condom commitment An agreement to confine exchange of bodily fluids and barrier-free intercourse to a closed group which has previously been screened for sexually transmitted diseases. *syn.* safe sex circle

Courting The process by which people explore how it feels to form or join in a committed relationship. *syn.* dating.

Cruising Attending activities solely to meet new partners and take them away with you without contributing anything to the group.

Group marriage A lovestyle in which three or more partners consciously chose to be primary with each other. Decisions are made by mutual consent. A group marriage may be open or closed. Sexual orientations may vary.

Grandfather A person who became your lover before you entered your current primary relationship.

Grex A synergistic group of highly interdependent individuals whose functioning is enhanced by their association.

Expanded family A lovestyle in which three or more partners consciously chose each other as family. Partners may or may not live together. There is the potential for all family members to be sexual with each other if they mutually chose to do so, but this is not a requirement for family membership. *Syn* intentional family.

Inclusive relationship A lovestyle in which all partners agree to include more lovers into their relationship.

Intimate network A polyamorous lovestyle in which several ongoing committed relationships coexist. There can be a mix of primary, secondary, and tertiary relationships. The structure may be parallel, circular, or web-like.

Lovestyle The design or structure of a sexualove relationship. Like the term lifestyle, it implies a conscious choice. *syn.* Relationship orientation.

Monogamy 1) A marriage in which two partners agree not to have sex or erotic love with anyone else. 2) A lovestyle for two players only.

Multipartner relationship Any nonmonogamous lovestyle.

New paradigm relating A philosophy of relationship which emphasizes using the relationship to consciously enhance the psychological and spiritual development of the partners. New paradigm relating is characterized by responding authentically in the present moment, honoring individual autonomy, equality, total honesty, and self responsibility.

Nonmonogamy A lovestyle which allows for more than one sexual relationship at a time.

Odd-one-out syndrome An intimate situation where one person feels left out, usually because there is an odd number of players.

Old paradigm relating A philosophy of relationship which emphasizes well defined rules, extensive agreements, ironclad conditions, and the importance of the group over the individual. Usually involves a hierarchical power structure.

Open marriage A marriage in which fidelity is not equated with monogamy.

Open relationship A lovestyle in which the partners have agreed that they can have sexual relations independently of each other.

Plural marriage A name often applied to Mormon-style polygyny. All the wives may live together, or each may have her own home.

Poly The relationship orientation of people who love and want to be intimate with more than one person at a time. Short for polyamory.

Polyamory A lovestyle which arises from the understanding that love can not be forced to flow, or not flow, in any particular direction. Polyamory emphasizes consciously choosing how many partners one wishes to engage with rather than accepting social norms which dictate loving only one person at a time. This is an umbrella term which includes open marriage, group marriage, expanded family, and intimate networks. It could also include intentional monogamy.

Polyandry A marriage with one wife and two or more husbands.

Polyfidelity 1) [original usage] a lovestyle in which three or more partners who are all primary with each other agree to be sexual only within their group. More primary partners can be added with everyone's consent. 2) [common usage] Polyamory, Responsible nonmonogamy.

Polygamy 1) A marriage which includes more than two people. A generic term which does not imply any particular configuration of partners. 2) A nonmonogamous lovestyle.

Polygyny A marriage with one husband and two or more wives.

Relationship orientation The preference for sexual relationships or lovestyles which are monogamous, nonmonogamous, inclusive, open, closed, casual, committed, serial, or polyfidelitous, etc. *syn.* Lovestyle.

Serial monogamy [originally **serial polygamy**] The most common lovestyle in the United States today. A form of *polyamory* which is limited to one partner at a time, with multiple partners over time.

Serial polyamory A form of polyamory in which one has a series of different primary partners while continuing to engage in various secondary and tertiary relationships.

Sexual orientation The preference for sexual partners of the same gender, opposite gender, either gender or both genders.

Spice Plural of spouse

Swinging Sport sex for couples. A form of monogamy in which two primary partners agree to have casual sex with other couples or singles as long as there is no emotional involvement.

Synergy The state of a system in which the whole is greater than the sum of its parts. Similar to *harmony* as expressed musically.

Triad Any three person lovestyle.

Trisexual The sexual orientation of a person who prefers to have sex with two or more other partners simultaneously.

ABOUT THE
LOVE WITHOUT LIMITS WORKSHOPS

The *Love Without Limits* workshops were created by Dr. Deborah Anapol in 1992 to provide an opportunity for both couples and singles to experience the paradigm shift in intimate relating. Taken as a whole our programs provide a powerful combination of polyamorous concepts, intimacy building experiences, relationship skills, spiritual communion, sexual healing and tantric practices.

Through breath, movement, hands-on healing, energy work, sharing from the heart, and spontaneous interaction we create an environment that supports you in letting go of old conditioning which prevents you from realizing the new possibilities for fulfilling connection with others. Thousands of people from coast to coast report that these powerfully transformational yet gently nurturing gatherings have changed their lives. We invite you to join us soon in creating community where the body is sacred, love is abundant, and the feminine is honored!

The *Love Without Limits* workshops are facilitated by Deborah Anapol, Ph.D. and a variety of friends and lovers. Dr. Anapol has a doctorate in clinical psychology from the University of Washington and has been working with individuals, families, and groups exploring new paradigm relating for over twenty years. She is available for phone consultation and private coaching by appointment only.

Love Without Limits has been featured on Donahue, Sally Jesse Raphael, Real Personal, and on TV and radio talk shows all across the country. **For information on upcoming events and publications,** or to arrange an event in your area **send a business size SASE to Dr. Deborah Anapol, POB 4322-L, San Rafael, CA 94913** or phone 415/507-1739. Email pad@well.com. **To order additional copies of *POLYAMORY: THE NEW LOVE WITHOUT LIMITS* send $16 plus $4 shipping and handling to the address above.**

PRAISE FOR

POLYAMORY: THE NEW LOVE WITHOUT LIMITS

"There are people of courage around to test the limits of various forms of cultural insanity, like conventional marriage, conventional war, and conventional politics. Deborah Anapol is such a person. Because she dares to do this she helps us face what we all say we want but we are all most terrified of: Love."

Brad Blanton, Ph.D., author Practicing Radical Honesty

"As a couple's counselor for many years I have seen how obligation poisons intimacy. In this ground breaking book Deborah Anapol shows us that there is another way to be intimate – a way that can lead us to freedom from the addiction to control."

Susan Campbell, Ph.D.
Author From Chaos to Confidence & Getting Real

"Exploring new paradigms, taking calculated risks and opening our hearts and minds is paramount to a conscious full life. A lifetime of knowledge, care, love, and professionalism has created this extraordinary work. This book is a primary resource for everyone exploring ways to have more truth, love and intimacy in their lives."

Suzie Heumann, founder of Tantra.com

"Combines compelling reasoning with language straight from the heart! Polyamory: The New Love Without Limits provides the first powerful intellectual and social framework for the lovestyle known as polyamory."

Dawson Church, author Facing Death & Finding Love

"Pioneering books like this one are helping us define new realities for ourselves. Deborah breaks down the barriers to thought and understanding that can stand between wanting to take a new approach to love and actually doing it. Once you've seen that others have crossed the territory, it's not so scary any more."

Eric Francis, Astrologer & Sex Educator

"Like it or not, we are in the midst of one of the greatest sexual revolutions in human history. It's frightening but exilarating. Monogamous, exclusive marriage was never the only way. Now we are freer to explore new, richer ways of bonding with others and creating families in the 21st century. This book is a clear and helpful guide to one important way a growing number of men and women are opening up and enriching their lives."

Robert Francoeur, Ph.D., author The International Encylopedia of Sex & Sex, Love, and Marriage in the 21st Century